Creative Activities for Gifted Readers

Grades 3–6

Dynamic Investigations, Challenging Projects, and Energizing Assignments

Anthony D. Fredericks

Good Year Books

Tucson, Arizona

To Richard Disher,
creative raconteur, gifted wit, and
one heck of a brother-in-law.

Good Year Books
Our titles are available for most basic curriculum subjects plus many enrichment areas. For more Good Year Books, contact your local bookseller or educational dealer. For a complete catalog with information about other Good Year Books, please contact:

Good Year Books
PO Box 91858
Tucson, AZ 85752-1858
www.goodyearbooks.com

Cover Design: Dan Miedaner
Text Design: Dan Miedaner
Drawings: Sean O'Neill

Portions of this book were previously printed in *The Gifted Reader Handbook.*

ISBN-10: 1-59647-109-3
ISBN-13: 978-1-59647-109-2

1 2 3 4 5 6 7 8 9 - MG - 13 12 11 10 09 08 07 06

Library of Congress Cataloging-in-Publication Data

Fredericks, Anthony D.
  Creative activities for gifted readers : dynamic investigations, challenging and energizing assignments / Anthony D. Fredericks.
    p. cm.
  ISBN-13: 978-1-59647-109-2
  ISBN-10: 1-59647-109-3
  1. Reading comprehension. 2. Gifted children--Education. 3. Activity programs in education. I. Title.

LB1573.7F74 2006
371.95'34--dc22

2006043468

Contents

Introduction

"The time has come," the Walrus said,
    "To talk of many things:
Of shoes—and ships—and sealing wax—
    Of cabbages—and kings—
And why the sea is boiling hot—
    And whether pigs have wings."
                    —*Lewis Carroll*

Gifted students present a unique challenge to elementary teachers. They are often the first ones done with a reading assignment or those who continually ask for more creative and interesting work. What these students frequently demand are ideas and materials that are not only challenging but relevant as well. What they need are exciting activities, energizing projects, and focused activity sheets that offer a creative curriculum within the framework of the regular reading program.

This book has been written with these gifted readers in mind. It contains a wide variety of ideas and suggestions designed to assist gifted children in developing the skills necessary to expand their reading horizons. A major focus of the book is to help children learn and apply the thinking and creative skills appropriate for reading competence. Assignments are offered that both extend the classroom reading program and help students explore the world around them.

Specifically, the objectives of this book are as follows:

1. Students will be involved in a facilitative learning process. They will be encouraged to plan and select assignments that meet their individual needs and interests. In turn, these self-directed explorations will lead to greater personal involvement and participation.

2. Students will learn to assume more responsibility for their own learning. In so doing, they will gain a greater awareness of their own abilities, develop a sense of self-direction, and improve their self-esteem.

3. Students will be exposed to a wide range of materials, assignments, and experiences—all designed to stimulate reading exploration above and beyond the basal text.

4. Divergent thinking skills will be emphasized in concert with creative endeavors. Thus, pupils will be encouraged to both process and interpret information. As a result, they will come to appreciate reading as a multifaceted subject.

5. Students will be able to explore reading beyond the walls of the classroom. By using their skills in practical and meaningful pursuits, they will gain a heightened awareness of their own competencies.

1

Each of the six units in this book focuses on six thinking skills and four creative extensions. The thinking skills include literal, reorganization, interpretive, evaluation, appreciation, and application. The four creative extensions are fluency, flexibility, originality, and elaboration.

Thinking Skills

1. *Literal.* The literal level of thinking involves the student's ability to locate, identify, recall, and remember specific facts in written material.

2. *Reorganization.* This refers to the ability to sort, group, or classify ideas into new patterns. Putting concepts or items into categories is one method of reorganization.

3. *Interpretive.* Using their own background of experiences, students develop inferences about story information. Making educational guesses is one use of interpretive skills.

4. *Evaluation.* Using a set of established criteria, students make personal judgments about the worth or merit of written material.

5. *Appreciation.* This refers to students' emotional responses to stories or books. It entails identifying affective reactions to written material.

6. *Application.* This skill focuses on students' ability to use information obtained from written sources in a variety of new situations.

Creative Extensions

1. *Fluency.* This is the ability to create a potpourri of ideas or lists of ideas. It involves the generation of many thoughts without regard to quality. Brainstorming is a good way to enhance fluency.

2. *Flexibility.* This skill involves drawing relationships between seemingly unrelated ideas (for example: "How is a rubber band like a dictionary?"). Locating common elements between items helps students look for many possible answers to a problem.

3. *Originality.* This refers to the creation of ideas that are singular and unique—those that are different from all others. It is the creative process we most often associate with gifted youngsters.

4. *Elaboration.* This is the process individuals go through to expand an idea—to enlarge it until it is workable or feasible. It is a process of addition or multiplication that builds ideas into their final form.

The assignments in this book have been developed in concert with varied groups of gifted youngsters. Many children have participated in the development of each activity sheet, activity, project, and story energizer, thus ensuring the relevancy of each assignment for all gifted readers. However, it is important that whichever assignments you select for your students, you take sufficient time to discuss the purpose of each one, in terms of both its immediate importance and its long-range implications. Providing opportunity for pupils to share and discuss the implications of these ideas for their own reading development will help them appreciate the selected assignments as a positive extension of their literacy development.

You are also encouraged to solicit follow-up activities from your gifted students. These units are not rigid; they can be modified and expanded as the dynamics of individuals or groups may warrant. When students have opportunities to extend and expand the ideas within each of these units, they will be able to see the value of their work in terms of long-range reading goals.

In short, the activity sheets, projects, activities, and story energizers in this book should serve as launching pads for students' imagination, thinking-skills development, and creativity enhancement.

The assignments are designed to be used in whatever order or sequence you feel to be most appropriate. You should plan to use a mix from the units throughout the year, providing varied opportunities for students to become actively involved in a selection of ideas, themes, and interests. In turn, their interest will be piqued and their motivation ensured.

This book has been written for the teacher who wishes to stimulate, encourage, and extend the learning opportunities for gifted readers. A healthy dose of these assignments within and throughout the reading program can produce pupils who are eager participants in the reading process. In turn, literacy growth can become an exciting and dynamic part of the world of gifted readers.

How to Use This Book

This book can be used in a variety of classrooms, grouping situations, or instructional formats. Here are some possibilities:

1. *The Regular Classroom.* All of the units can be used in a regular classroom containing both gifted and on-level readers. As such, units can be assigned (a) when scheduled reading assignments have been completed, (b) in place of regular assignments, or (c) as supplemental work to strengthen concepts presented in the reading curriculum.

2. *Special Gifted Class.* This book presents a number of options for special gifted classes. These include (a) using the units in addition to the regular reading curriculum, (b) developing a complete reading curriculum for gifted pupils based on these assignments, or (c) scheduling individual or small-group work as an extension of previously learned concepts and skills.

3. *At Home.* Parents will find these assignments appropriate for home use, too. Each unit focuses on a variety of thinking skills and creative extensions, using a nonthreatening format that families can enjoy together. Parents should treat these ideas as fun-to-do assignments rather than as graded work. It is important, therefore, that the atmosphere be low-key, relaxed, and informal—enjoyment should be the watchword. Total family involvement will help gifted students apply classroom-learned skills in a variety of practical situations.

This book can be used in a variety of ways, depending on individual classroom dynamics and on the instructional plans you wish to emphasize. In choosing assignments for your gifted students, you may wish to give some thought to the following:

1. Try a variety of grouping strategies. Most of the activity sheets, activities, projects, and story energizers can be done as individual or as small-group work. Provide children with a selection of sharing opportunities, too.

2. All of the units are nongraded. However, you may wish to set up your own evaluation system or have students help in establishing appropriate evaluation criteria. This will ensure maximum pupil involvement—a factor that enhances both cognitive and affective development.

3. There is no set order or sequence to the assignments. You are free to choose appropriate work or allow students a measure of self-selection in determining the assignments they would like to pursue.

4. Whatever activity sheets, activities, projects, or story energizers you or your students select, it will be important to keep time limits flexible. Suggested completion times are included in the introduction to each unit but are offered as approximations only. After students have completed several assignments, you will be able to judge appropriate time limits for future work.

5. Most of the units require either some degree of student independence or an extended period of time for completion. Consequently, it is strongly suggested that you schedule periodic conferences with individual students or with small groups of students. These conferences can provide you with an opportunity to gauge student progress and discuss issues or concerns specific to individual assignments.

Assignment Scheduling

Following is a suggested plan for assigning individual lessons within each unit. Feel free to modify it according to the dynamics or time limitations of your classes.

1. Introduce an assignment or lesson to individuals or small groups. Be sure to provide a complete list of all the necessary requirements.

2. Have students discuss several options for completing an assignment. Make sure discussion centers on how the assignment will be initiated, pursued, and terminated.

3. Give students plenty of time to examine several assignments thoroughly and to make their own choices. Students may opt to work on specific lessons individually or in small groups.

4. Have students begin working on selected activity sheets, activities, projects, or story energizers.

5. Allow students sufficient time to plan culminating projects or presentations. Have them set a target date for completion of a selected assignment.

6. Provide opportunities to share the results of an assignment, to discuss its implications, and to evaluate the product(s).

Reporting Formats

As students complete the individual activity sheets, activities, projects, or story energizers, they will want to report their newly discovered information. The list on page 6 contains several possibilities for sharing student information with other class members as well as with you. You should encourage students to select a variety of reporting formats throughout the year and throughout the assignments.

The variety of instructional options and reporting formats guarantees that students will be able to discover many exciting dimensions to the world of reading. In so doing, they will have the opportunity to use their classroom skills in varied literary explorations beyond the classroom.

book reviews
illustrated talks
posters
poems
chalk talks
brochures
dramas
folders
games
panoramas
mobiles
discussion groups
murals
dioramas
maps
dances
shadowboxes
collections
lists
Web pages
PowerPoint presentations
blogs (as appropriate)
e-mail communiqués (as appropriate)

booklets
videos
file boxes
recordings
charts
bulletin boards
cartoons
sculptures
pantomimes
book jackets
reference books
roller movies
time lines
puppets
puzzles
PA announcements
activity sheets
songs
CDs
Webquests

storytelling
carvings
clay models
book talks
advertisements
scripts
filmstrips
guidebooks
displays
diaries
drawings
news articles
scrapbooks
models
letters to authors
collages
flannel boards
bookmarks
Videodisks
iTunes

Puzzles and Problems

Independent learning has long been a hallmark of gifted reading instruction. This first unit offers gifted students a number of motivating activity sheets designed to challenge them in a variety of reading areas, to encourage them in the development of both reading and creative skills, and to provide them with opportunities for individual exploration of selected interest areas.

You can reproduce each activity sheet and give it to students. Each emphasizes at least two thinking skills and is designed to reinforce and extend students' cognitive processes. Although this section can often be completed without additional reference materials, encourage students to engage in extra research whenever necessary, using a multitude of classroom or library resources. This option stimulates students to experience and appreciate the universality of reading in their lives.

Students should be able to finish each activity sheet in one or two class periods. Each can be completed independently or by a small group of two or three students. You can use the activity sheets in any order. You may wish to use them upon completion of a regular reading assignment, as an element in a guided reading lesson, as a separate assignment, or as a special homework paper.

In all, the activity sheets offer students opportunities to develop thinking skills in a fun, interesting, and meaningful format. Sprinkled liberally throughout the reading curriculum, they can add a touch of spice to gifted students' development as well-rounded readers.

Color My World

Name _____

Date _____

Directions:

Many words and phrases in our language include color words. For example, the word *greenbacks* means dollar bills or money. Locate and write a definition for each of the following colorful words and phrases:

red tape _____

golden rule _____

yellowjacket _____

blacktop _____

blue chip _____

silver lining _____

yellow streak _____

white elephant _____

red alert _____

blackmail _____

silversmith _____

blue bloods _____

whitewash _____

Directions:

For each of the definitions below, locate a colorful word or phrase:

Highest rank in tae kwon do _____

Place where plants are grown _____

Girl who visited the three bears _____

Heated to a very high temperature _____

Something an expert gardener is said to have _____

The brain _____

A novice _____

A tropical disease _____

To edit a manuscript _____

To be sad _____

Special grass in Kentucky _____

Begin and End

Name _____

Date _____

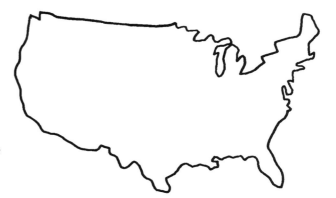

Thinking Skills
• Literal
• Reorganization
• Application

Directions:

There are lots of words that begin and end with the same letter. Look at each of the categories below. See how many words you can create in each category. Give yourself a time limit (10 minutes, for example) and see how you do. An example has been provided for each category.

Words that begin and end with A	Words that begin and end with N	Words that begin and end with R
1. America	1. Neutron	1. Regular
2.	2.	2.
3.	3.	3.
4.	4.	4.
5.	5.	5.
6.	6.	6.
7.	7.	7.
8.	8.	8.
9.	9.	9.
10.	10.	10.

Words that begin and end with D	Words that begin and end with P	Words that begin and end with L
1. Dead	1. Pump	1. Label
2.	2.	2.
3.	3.	3.
4.	4.	4.
5.	5.	5.
6.	6.	6.
7.	7.	7.
8.	8.	8.
9.	9.	9.
10.	10.	10.

Word Whip

Name _____

Date _____

Thinking Skills
- Literal
- Reorganization

Directions:

Find the names of eighteen animals in the puzzle below (words go across or down). Then write the animal names in the correct column at the bottom of the sheet.

A	E	O	P	C	H	I	C	K	E	N	D
P	H	G	I	R	A	F	F	E	J	Z	U
F	O	O	G	M	R	O	O	S	T	E	R
C	R	O	C	O	D	I	L	E	I	B	T
O	S	S	N	N	U	M	H	B	L	R	H
W	E	E	Y	K	C	A	M	E	L	A	I
L	I	O	N	E	K	E	D	A	A	K	P
Q	R	G	A	Y	S	X	O	R	M	W	P
B	Z	L	A	M	B	C	G	V	A	L	O

Farm Animals

_____

_____

_____

_____

_____

_____

_____

_____

_____

Zoo Animals

_____

_____

_____

_____

_____

_____

_____

_____

_____

UNIT ONE: PUZZLES AND PROBLEMS

Animals Inside

Name _____

Date _____

Thinking Skills
• Literal
• Reorganization

Directions:

There are many words that have smaller words hidden inside them. Look at each of the animals listed in the left-hand column below. Try to think of as many words as you can that have the name of that animal hidden inside each one. An example has been provided for each animal.

A. Words that contain **ant**	1. f<u>ant</u>asy 2. 3. 4. 5.
B. Words that contain **hen**	1. t<u>hen</u> 2. 3. 4. 5.
C. Words that contain **fish**	1. sel<u>fish</u> 2. 3. 4. 5..
D. Words that contain **fly**	1. butter<u>fly</u> 2. 3. 4. 5.
E. Words that contain **rat**	1. <u>rat</u>tle 2. 3. 4. 5.

Mixed-up Words

Thinking Skills
• Literal
• Reorganization

Name _____

Date _____

Directions:

An anagram is a word with letters that can be arranged to form another word. For example, the letters in CARE can be rearranged to form the word RACE. For each of the words below, move the letters around to form a new word:

seat _____

read _____

robe _____

reed _____

spin _____

coast _____

rat _____

oars _____

mate _____

keep _____

star _____

spray _____

net _____

meal _____

span _____

part _____

words _____

bear _____

grab _____

steam _____

trap _____

lane _____

pear _____

lap _____

In the Right Order

Name _____

Date _____

Directions:

Look at the following sentence:

Coach **d**esigned **e**ach **f**ootball **g**ame **h**appily.

Notice how the first word in the sentence begins with the letter **c**. Then the next word begins with **d**—the next letter in the alphabet. Then the next letter begins with **e**—the next letter in the alphabet . . . and so on. Each word begins with the letter that follows the letter that began the previous word.

For each letter in the first box below, create a sequence sentence. The first word starts with the designated letter, then each following word must start with the next letter in the alphabet. After you have done the first box, try the challenges in the next two boxes.

1. A _____ .

2. M _____ .

3. R _____ .

A **four**-word sentence:
   C _____ .

A **five**-word sentence:
   N _____ .

A **six**-word sentence:
   H _____ .

A **seven**-word sentence:
   L _____ .

A sentence of **ten** words or more _____
_____

Animal Farm

Directions:

There are many things to learn about animals. One of the most interesting is the groups to which animals belong. For example, you probably know about a **pride** of lions, a **flock** of birds, and a **school** of fish. But there are other names of groups (known as collective nouns) to which animals belong. See if you can complete the following (the first one has been done for you):

An **army** of ____caterpillars____

A **nide** of _____

A **bob** of _____

An **ostentation** of _____

A **crash** of _____

A **pod** of _____

A **drift** of _____

A **quiver** of _____

An **earth** of _____

A **rhumba** of _____

A **family** of _____

A **smack** of _____

A **glint** of _____

A **tower** of _____

A **hatch** of _____

An **ugly** of _____

An **intrusion** of _____

A **volery** of _____

A **jug** of _____

A **wisp** of _____

A **knot** of _____

An **exaltation** of _____

A **lounge** of _____

A **yoke** of _____

A **murder** of _____

A **zeal** of _____

Can you locate the group names for the following animals? The first one has been done for you:

tigers ____ambush____

turtles _____

worms _____

woodpeckers _____

bees _____

piglets _____

geese _____

penguins _____

UNIT ONE: PUZZLES AND PROBLEMS

One More Time

Name _____

Date _____

Directions:

Each item below has a series of four words. Each series is in a particular pattern. Figure out the pattern and add one more word that continues the pattern. Afterward, explain what the pattern is.

Example:

A . . . by . . . cat . . . dare . . . _____early_____

   Why? The next word must have five letters and begin with the next letter in the alphabet.

1. Carl . . . Linda . . . Ann . . . Ned . . . _____

   Why? _____

2. zebra . . . yellow . . . x ray . . . water . . . _____

   Why? _____

3. I . . . in . . . imp . . . idea . . . _____

   Why? _____

4. merry . . . noble . . . often . . . place . . . _____

   Why? _____

5. stare . . . rat . . . are . . . rest . . . _____

   Why? _____

Puzzle Me

Name _____

Date _____

Directions:

There are many different types of word puzzles. The ones here allow you to use any letters you wish to complete each diagram. But be careful—they're not as easy as they look!

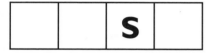

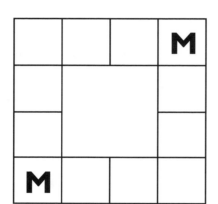
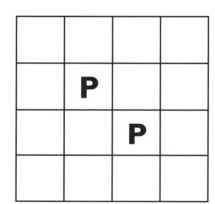

UNIT ONE: PUZZLES AND PROBLEMS

Add One More

Name _____

Date _____

Directions:

Write a sentence on each line below. Each sentence must begin with a three-letter word. The next word in each sentence must be four letters long. The next word must be five letters long, and so on. What is the longest sentence you can create?

Example:

The open house really exposed everyone.

1. _____ .

2. _____ .

3. _____ .

4. _____ .

5. _____ .

6. _____ .

7. _____ .

8. _____ .

Crazy Headlines

Name _____

Date _____

Directions:

Each imaginary newspaper headline below describes a Mother Goose rhyme. Decipher each one using a dictionary, thesaurus, or Mother Goose treasury.

1. Nimble Lad Bounds Over Conflagration

   _____

2. Jolly Ruler Obtains Necessary Items

   _____

3. Azure Youth Found Napping

   _____

4. Youth Osculates Unwilling Maidens

   _____

5. Children's Group Encircles Solitary Shrub

   _____

6. Bovine Clears Earth's Satellite

   _____

7. Rodent Ascends Timepiece

   _____

8. Royal Experts Face Scrambled Mess

   _____

9. Elderly Gentleman Knocked Out During Downpour

   _____

10. Youthful Pair Injured on Knoll

    _____

11. Maiden Loses Tailless Flock

    _____

12. Strange Fruit Discovered in Pastry

    _____

13. British Edifice Seen Collapsing

    _____

14. Frightful Arachnid Bothers Young Woman

    _____

15. Young Sheep Causes Panic at Local School

    _____

16. Elderly Housewife and Canine Face Starvation

    _____

17. Pastry Maker Hurries to Complete Special Order

    _____

A Man, a Plan, a Canal: Panama!

From *Creative Activities for Gifted Readers, 3–6* © Good Year Books. This page may be reproduced for classroom use only by the actual purchaser of the book. www.goodyearbooks.com

Thinking Skills
- Literal
- Reorganization

Name _____

Date _____

Directions:

A palindrome is a word, phrase, verse or sentence that reads the same backward and forward. (The title of this activity sheet is a palindrome—it reads the same forward and backward. Go ahead, try it!)

In each box below, create as many palindromes as you can (examples have been provided for you). You may wish to challenge another student and see who can create the most palindromes in a designated time limit (fifteen minutes, for example).

Names:

Otto _____   _____   _____

Eve _____   _____   _____

Objects/Items:

kayak _____   _____   _____

noon _____   _____   _____

_____   _____   _____

Phrases/Sentences:

Evil olive   Ten animals did slam in a net.
Top spot   Ma has a ham.

_____

_____

_____

_____

_____

_____

Up, Down, and Across

Name _____

Date _____

Directions:

The name of a popular chapter book is hidden in each of the boxes below. With your pencil, begin in the upper left corner and move from letter to letter to trace the answer. You may move up, down, or sideways, but you cannot use a letter more than once or cross your path. Keep in mind that you may not need to use all the letters.

1.

J	T	S	A	M	C	H
A	M	E	N	E	A	C
U	H	T	D	P	T	Q
P	E	G	I	A	N	A
S	G	E	T	F	D	B

3.

W	P	H	E	M	T
H	E	T	R	V	C
E	R	E	E	W	S
B	E	F	D	O	D
N	R	N	G	R	O

2.

A	W	R	B
G	H	I	N
I	E	L	K
N	T	E	F
D	I	M	C

4.

H	T	T	E	R	B
A	O	P	R	A	S
R	R	Y	D	N	T
A	H	H	T	D	E
M	C	E	F	S	R
B	E	R	O	E	C

Your Order Please I

Thinking Skills
• Literal
• Reorganization

Name _____

Date _____

Directions:

Four of the five sentences in each set below are not in the correct order (one sentence does not belong with the other four). Write the numbers 1, 2, 3, or 4 before the sentences to indicate the right order (one sentence will be left blank).

1. _____ Food then passes through the small intestine.

_____ It travels to the left side of the heart.

_____ After being chewed, food passes down your esophagus.

_____ While food is in the stomach, acids begin to break it down.

_____ The chemical particles can then pass into the bloodstream.

2. _____ The brain flashes a response along the motor nerves.

_____ Oxygen is exhaled from the lungs.

_____ The nerve ending is stimulated.

_____ The message reaches the brain.

_____ The message is sent along sensory nerves to the spinal cord.

3. _____ It then moves through the larynx to the trachea.

_____ Air is taken in through the nose and hollow nasal passages to be warmed and filtered.

_____ There the air goes to the two bronchial tubes that are attached to each lung.

_____ Blood is pumped from the heart to the lungs.

_____ The tiny balloon-like sacs are filled with air.

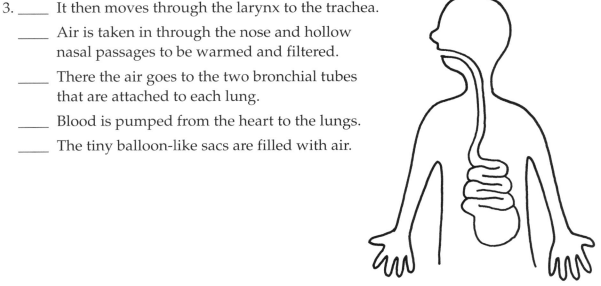

Pyramid Sentences

Name _____

Date _____

Directions:

Sentences can be as long or as short as you wish. In this exercise you will construct a series of sentences, each one word longer than the previous one. Each new sentence must begin with the same letter and must use at least one word from the sentence above it. Here is an example:

Target word: dogs

> Dogs dig.
> Dangerous dogs dig.
> Delightful dogs dig dirt.
> Dogs digging dirt dig daily.

Target word: cats

_____

_____

_____

_____

Target word: mothers

_____

_____

_____

_____

Target word: books

_____

_____

_____

_____

Target word: teachers

_____

_____

_____

_____

MEET ME BY THE SPHINX

Sentence Challenge I

Thinking Skills
- Literal
- Reorganization

Name _____

Date _____

Directions:

On each line below, create a sentence that follows the specific rule. Make sure each sentence is more than four words long.

1. A sentence that does not have the letter **r** in it

   _____

2. A sentence in which every word begins with a vowel

   _____

3. A sentence in which every word ends with an **s**

   _____

4. A sentence in which every word has a double consonant (tt, dd)

   _____

5. A sentence that does not have a long vowel

   _____

6. A sentence in which every word has the letter **t**

   _____

Answer First

Name _____

Date _____

Directions:

For each number below, there are two answers. Compose two sentences that could be answered by both of the items.

Example:

Answers: **dogs   cats**

A. What are two four-legged animals?

B. What are two different kinds of mammals?

1. Answers: **hurricanes   tornadoes**

   A. _____

   B. _____

2. Answers: **DVD   CD**

   A. _____

   B. _____

3. Answers: **Mexico   Australia**

   A. _____

   B. _____

4. Answers: **pumpkin   wreath**

   A. _____

   B. _____

What's Right? I

Name _____

Date _____

Directions:

Read all four sentences in each group. Then
circle the one correct statement in each group.

All plants need food.
Every plant has some green coloring.
All plants have leaves and stems.
Oxygen and carbon dioxide are by-products of all plants.

Living things are composed of cells.
Plant and animal cells are alike.
The chromosomes are found in the cytoplasm.
Blood is stored in the vacuoles.

A lever is used to push a load.
An inclined plane is used to pull a load.
A screw is used to push a load.
A pulley is used to pull a load.

Magma comes from the Earth's crust.
Earthquakes are movements of rock in the Earth's mantle.
Volcanoes push hot rock up from the Earth's core.
Earthquakes always happen on land or above sea level.

Rain, snow, and sleet are the only forms of precipitation.
Clouds form when warm, moist air cools.
Fog occurs only near lakes, rivers, or streams.
Solar energy changes water vapor into water.

In Short

Name _____

Date _____

Directions:

Each of the words listed below is the shortened form of a longer word. For example, the word *gym* is the shortened form of the word *gymnasium*. For each "short" word below, write its longer form.

1. taxi _____

2. burger _____

3. auto _____

4. exam _____

5. bike _____

6. plane _____

7. gas _____

8. vet _____

9. sub _____

10. math _____

11. ref _____

12. champ _____

Challenge:

Create a sentence that has at least four of the words above.

_____

_____

Your Order Please II

Name _____

Date _____

Directions:

Four of the five geographical terms or sentences in each set below are not in the correct order. A fifth does not belong with the other four. Write the numbers 1, 2, 3, or 4 before each to indicate the right order. Leave the unrelated sentence or word blank.

1. _____ It flows past St. Louis.

   _____ It flows across Illinois.

   _____ It meets with the Ohio River.

   _____ It is part of the border of Minnesota.

   _____ It is part of the border of Louisiana.

2. _____ Cool air masses meet with clouds.

   _____ Warm air masses settle in low-lying areas.

   _____ Water is changed into water vapor.

   _____ Condensation occurs over large bodies of water.

   _____ Clouds form over land masses.

The world's tallest mountains are:

3. _____ Lhotse I

   _____ Kanchenjunga

   _____ Mt. Everest

   _____ Matterhorn

   _____ K2

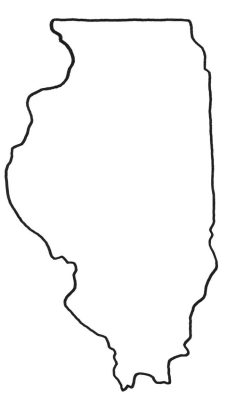

The Right Size

Name _____

Date _____

Directions:

One way to think about the meaning of words is to put them in order according to the size of the objects they name. For example, "nickel, shirt, boat, ocean" would be in the correct order because a shirt is bigger than a nickel, a boat is bigger than a shirt, and an ocean is bigger than a boat. Put the following groups of words in the correct order from smallest to largest.

1. house   seed   nail   mouse

   _____

2. elephant   dime   toaster   tire

   _____

3. lantern   worm   apple   hill

   _____

4. elevator   speck   desk   light bulb

   _____

5. cup   automobile   blanket   circus

   _____

6. pencil   school   table   book

   _____

7. shoe   doughnut   elm   tuba

   _____

8. donkey   bee   bird   folder

   _____

Directions:

Now put these words in order from largest item to smallest.

1. sock   ant   octopus   river

   _____

2. robot   potato   pearl   squirrel

   _____

3. envelope   record   aunt   train

   _____

4. jacket   bridge   necklace   chair

   _____

5. menu   city   wagon   mayor

   _____

6. pocket   porcupine   dictionary   finger

   _____

7. postcard   staple   gym   shark

   _____

8. calendar   forest   carnation   key

   _____

UNIT ONE: PUZZLES AND PROBLEMS

Sentence Challenge II

Thinking Skills
- Literal
- Reorganization

Name _____

Date _____

Directions:

Create a sentence on each line below that follows the specific rule. Make sure each sentence is more than four words long.

1. A sentence that does not have the letter **s** in it

   _____

2. A sentence in which every word begins with the letter **r**

   _____

3. A sentence in which every word begins and ends with an **s**

   _____

4. A sentence in which every word begins with the last letter of the previous word

   _____

5. A sentence in which the words are in reverse alphabetical order

   _____

6. A sentence in which every word has one less letter than the previous word

   _____

Fantastic Food

Name _____

Date _____

Directions:

Foods can be put into many categories. On the line in front of each food item below, write the letters of the food categories to which it can belong. The first one has been done for you.

A. vegetable
B. green
C. fruit
D. red
E. sweet
F. sour
G. grows on trees
H. grows in the ground
I. meat

_B, C, D, E, H_   1. strawberry

_____   2. apple

_____   3. corn

_____   4. potato

_____   5. lettuce

_____   6. lime

_____   7. tomato

_____   8. hamburger

_____   9. ice cream

_____   10. rice

_____   11. grapes

_____   12. ham

_____   13. celery

_____   14. peas

_____   15. pumpkin

_____   16. walnut

_____   17. raspberry

_____   18. chocolate

_____   19. lemon

_____   20. peanut

What's Right? II

Name _____

Date _____

Thinking Skills
• Literal
• Reorganization

Directions:

Read all four sentences in each group. Then circle the one correct statement in each group.

Hawaii is farther south than Florida.
Iowa is farther east than Arkansas.
Kentucky is farther north than Kansas.
Nebraska is farther west than Texas.

Four states border California.
Eight states border Missouri.
Three states border North Carolina.
Four states border West Virginia.

NE is the opposite of SW.
SE is the opposite of NE.
NW is the opposite of SW.
SW is the opposite of SE.

One mile = 1,760 yards
One mile = 22,240 inches
One mile = 1.7 kilometers
One mile = 390 meters

Columbia and Chad are in the Western Hemisphere.
Australia and Argentina are in the Southern Hemisphere.
Bolivia and Bulgaria are in the Eastern Hemisphere.
Mongolia and Malaysia are in the Northern Hemisphere.

By Ones and Two

Name _____

Date _____

Directions:

Many words in our language have the sound of numbers in them. For example: today (two-day). By "adding one" to those "numbers" you can create an *inflated word*. For example: "today" becomes "threeday." For each of the inflated words below, "subtract one" and write the normal spelling. Then put the normal words on a diet by "subtracting one" again and writing the "reduced" word.

DON'T FIVEGET ME!

Example: sometwo   _____ someone _____   _____ somezero _____

fivek	_____	_____
threeword	_____	_____
fivetune	_____	_____
elevennis	_____	_____
twoderful	_____	_____
crenine	_____	_____
elevension	_____	_____
grnine	_____	_____
lniner	_____	_____
Califivenia	_____	_____
Elevennessee	_____	_____
tomnineo	_____	_____

Directions:

Decode the sentences below by subtracting where necessary.

1. Threeday I'm going three the store five a crnine of apples.

   _____

2. Twoce upon a time three pirates buried a fivetune of pieces of nine.

   _____

3. Threesday was twoderful, except I was lnine five my fiveeign language class.

   _____

4. I twoder if the threetor will fiveget the sixteen books about the seventies and eighties.

   _____

Construction Junction

From *Creative Activities for Gifted Readers, 3–6* © Good Year Books. This page may be reproduced for classroom use only by the actual purchaser of the book. www.goodyearbooks.com

Thinking Skills
- Literal
- Reorganization

Name _____

Date _____

Directions:

For each number below there are several blanks. Use the blanks to create a sentence (five blanks = a five-word sentence). Please note that for each number there are letters placed at the beginning or end of selected blanks. You must use those letters in constructing words for each of your sentences.

Example:

_____ s _____ b _____ _____ _____ .

Bob's   sister   brought   six   cookies.

1. _____ r _____ r _____ _____ .

2. C _____ _____ s _____ _____ _____ .

3. _____ s _____ s _____ s _____ s _____ .

4. _____ e _____ e _____ _____ d.

5. A _____ b _____ c _____ d _____ e _____ .

6. S _____ s s _____ _____ s s _____ s.

7. ___ e ___ ___ e ___ ___ e ___ ___ e ___ ___ e ___ .

8. _____ m m _____ _____ m m _____ .

The Right Place

Thinking Skills
- Reorganization
- Application

Name _____

Date _____

Directions:

Learning about the categories or groups that words belong to can be an interesting part of vocabulary work. Look up the following words in the dictionary and write each under one of the proper categories below.

kimono	surrey	ark	legume	serape	sapling
sandal	fluid	julep	seltzer	lentil	trapeze
monorail	nectar	snood	yam	conifer	orchid
fern	epaulet	lace	blimp	equine	locomotive
pachyderm	coach	cola	libation	cordial	ornament

Drink It	Wear It	Ride It	Plant It

UNIT ONE: PUZZLES AND PROBLEMS

Front and Back

From *Creative Activities for Gifted Readers, 3–6* © Good Year Books. This page may be reproduced for classroom use only by the actual purchaser of the book. www.goodyearbooks.com

Name _____

Date _____

Directions:

For each blank below, write a word that begins with the first letter and ends with the last letter. Try to form as many words as you can. You may wish to challenge a friend and see who can create the most words within a certain time limit (fifteen minutes, for example).

Note: You may not be able to create words for all of the blanks.

A	_____	A		A	_____	B	
B	_____	B		B	_____	C	
C	_____	C		C	_____	D	
D	_____	D		D	_____	E	
E	_____	E		E	_____	F	
F	_____	F		F	_____	G	
G	_____	G		G	_____	H	
H	_____	H		H	_____	I	
I	_____	I		I	_____	J	
J	_____	J		J	_____	K	
K	_____	K		K	_____	L	
L	_____	L		L	_____	M	
M	_____	M		M	_____	N	
N	_____	N		N	_____	O	
O	_____	O		O	_____	P	
P	_____	P		P	_____	Q	
Q	_____	Q		Q	_____	R	
R	_____	R		R	_____	S	
S	_____	S		S	_____	T	
T	_____	T		T	_____	U	
U	_____	U		U	_____	V	
V	_____	V		V	_____	W	
W	_____	W		W	_____	X	
X	_____	X		X	_____	Y	
Y	_____	Y		Y	_____	Z	
Z	_____	Z		Z	_____	A	

Making Cents

Name _____

Date _____

Directions:

This exercise is based on a secret code in which each letter of the alphabet has its own price. Based on the costs of each of the words below, try to figure out the code. Then complete the code box at right. Afterward, solve the word problems under the box.

no	=	29¢		
sky	=	55¢		
hi	=	17¢		
yes	=	49¢		
bad	=	7¢		
face	=	15¢		
cat	=	24¢		
is	=	28¢		

A = _____	N = _____
B = _____	O = _____
C = _____	P = _____
D = _____	Q = _____
E = _____	R = _____
F = _____	S = _____
G = _____	T = _____
H = _____	U = _____
I = _____	V = _____
J = _____	W = _____
K = _____	X = _____
L = _____	Y = _____
M = _____	Z = _____

What is the price of your first name? _____

What is the price of your last name? _____

What is the most expensive letter in your whole name? _____

What is the price of "oranges"? _____

What is the price of "apples"? _____

Which is cheaper, "cookies" or "candy"?

_____

UNIT ONE: PUZZLES AND PROBLEMS

Who Said That?

Name _____

Date _____

Directions:

Listed below are some sayings that could have been said by story characters but were not. Match each saying with the character who could have said it.

1. "I think some dynamite will take care of this house."

2. "I could probably get to Grandma's house faster with a motorcycle."

3. "The next time that spider comes around, I'm going to smash him."

4. "If I only had a vacuum cleaner, I could keep this house clean."

5. "If I had more power, I could make it up this hill easily."

6. "I could move into a cave so no one would ever see me."

7. "I think I'll take a little nap."

8. "I like to fly with my friends."

9. "I don't always listen to mother."

10. "The forest is so quiet and yet still full of adventure."

_____ Peter Rabbit

_____ Cinderella

_____ Sleeping Beauty

_____ Red Riding Hood's Wolf

_____ The Ugly Duckling

_____ Bambi

_____ Big Bad Wolf

_____ Little Miss Muffet

_____ The Little Engine That Could

_____ Peter Pan

Simile Swing

Name _____

Date _____

Directions:

Many expressions add color and spice to what we read by making comparisons with familiar parts of the world around us. Look up the meaning of the word *simile* and then complete each of the common expressions below with the name of an animal or object.

Funny as a _____

Busy as a _____

Fast as a _____

Cool as a _____

Near as a _____

Happy as a _____

Sly as a _____

Red as a _____

Sharp as a _____

Strong as a _____

Light as a _____

Proud as a _____

Directions:

Now, create some original expressions of your own using the following sentence stems:

The jet was as loud as _____

_____

The haunted house was as scary as _____

_____

The crowd was as wild as _____

_____

The car was as fast as _____

_____

The clock was as old as _____

_____

Grandfather was as sleepy as_____

_____

UNIT ONE: PUZZLES AND PROBLEMS

What's That?

Name _____

Date _____

Directions:
There are many popular sayings that people use all the time, such as "It's a tough job but somebody's got to do it" and "Absence makes the heart grow fonder." The following sayings have been altered by substituting synonyms for familiar words. Can you translate them all?

1. Scintillate, Scintillate, celestial objective minified

   _____
   _____

2. Members of an avian species of identical plumage congregate.

   _____
   _____

3. Investigate prior to saltation.

   _____
   _____

4. Refrain from becoming lachrymose over precipitately departed lacteal fluid.

   _____
   _____

5. The stylus is more potent than the claymore.

   _____
   _____

6. It is fruitless to attempt to indoctrinate a superannuated canine with innovative maneuvers.

   _____
   _____

7. Eschew the implement of correction and coddle the scion.

   _____
   _____

8. Where there are visible vapors having their provenance in ignited carbonaceous materials, there is conflagration.

   _____
   _____

9. A plethora of individuals with expertise in culinary techniques vitiates the potable concoction produced by steeping certain comestibles.

   _____
   _____

10. Male cadavers are incapable of yielding any testimony.

   _____
   _____

What's in a Name?

Name _____

Date _____

Directions:

Match the imaginary book titles listed below with their imaginary authors. Put the number of the title in front of its appropriate "author."

Title	Author
1. *The Terrible Day*	___ C. U. Later
2. *Waiting in Line*	___ Ima Hogg
3. *How to Teach Reading*	___ I. M. Sadd
4. *My Favorite Bird*	___ Page Turner
5. *Sprinting around the Track*	___ Noah Lott
6. *Taking a Trip*	___ C. Howie Runns
7. *Crawling through the Desert*	___ Willie Makeit
8. *How to Increase Your IQ*	___ Jack O'Diamonds
9. *How to Gain Weight*	___ S. Lois Molassis
10. *Winning at Cards*	___ E. Z. Duzitt
11. *The Mardi Gras*	___ Ima Sparrow
12. *Fifty Years in the Classroom*	___ Newell Leans
13. *Fancy Desserts*	___ N. Struckter
14. *Make a Million without Working*	___ Pat E. Kaike

Directions:

Make up some "authors" for the following titles:

Up in the Mountains _____

Learning to Drive _____

Furry Animals _____

Sailing Made Easy _____

Working with Wood _____

A Day at the Park _____

All about the Library _____

Be Physically Fit _____

More Than One

Name _____

Date _____

Directions:

Many words have more than one meaning. For each word below, write two different ways it could be used or defined. The first one has been done for you.

___travel___	fly	___insect___
_____	bat	_____
_____	coat	_____
_____	horn	_____
_____	slip	_____
_____	roll	_____
_____	trip	_____
_____	foot	_____
_____	bark	_____
_____	ring	_____
_____	pen	_____

Directions:

For each set of words below, write one word that is related to both of the other words. The first one has been done for you.

drama	___play___	game
season	_____	coil
orchestra	_____	gather
flower	_____	ascended
locomotive	_____	exercise
memo	_____	music
carnival	_____	reasonable
weight	_____	hit
shrub	_____	factory
carton	_____	fight
tool	_____	viewed

Hinky Pinkys

Name _____

Date _____

Directions:

A Hinky Pinky is a two-word rhyming definition to a riddle. For example: A "foolish William" is a "silly Billy." Notice that the first word of the rhyming definition is an adjective, and the second one is a noun. Try writing hinky pinkys for each of the following riddles:

1. A fast hen

   _____   _____

2. A sneaky boy

   _____   _____

3. A small wasp

   _____   _____

4. Lemon gelatin

   _____   _____

5. A fat cement block

   _____   _____

6. A seafood platter

   _____   _____

7. A girl from Switzerland

   _____   _____

8. A sneaky insect

   _____   _____

9. A happy father

   _____   _____

10. An honest rabbit

   _____   _____

Directions:

Write riddles that could be used for each of the following hinky pinkys. For example: "a fried bride" might be "a cooked newlywed."

1. A <u>shook crook</u> is

   _____

2. A <u>cross boss</u> is

   _____

3. A <u>dope soap</u> is

   _____

4. A <u>dark ark</u> is

   _____

5. A <u>flower shower</u> is

   _____

6. A <u>blue shoe</u> is

   _____

7. A <u>bored board</u> is

   _____

8. A <u>fair pair</u> is

   _____

9. <u>Nice ice</u> is

   _____

10. A <u>dead bed</u> is

   _____

Word Wizards

Word Wizards are puzzles that encourage gifted students to use both deductive (going from the general to the specific) and inductive (going from the specific to the general) reasoning skills. These puzzles are an excellent way to help gifted students see the value of problem solving in a host of language arts activities. Above all, Word Wizards emphasize logic—encouraging students to analyze a problem, examine information, evaluate possible solutions, explore possibilities, and follow a sequence of steps in order to arrive at a solution.

Equally important is an emphasis on creative thinking. In each of these puzzles students will be able to use (and understand the applications of) fluency, flexibility, originality, and elaboration with the words, phrases, colloquialisms, terminology and vocabulary of our language. Both divergent and creative thinking is underscored in a "code" that students solve in a fun and engaging way. In short, there is no one "right way" to solve a particular problem—students have the option (and should be encouraged) to use a multiplicity of problem-solving skills and abilities.

Use a variety of the following strategies in the work you assign or create for your gifted students:

- Provide individual students or a small group of students with a complete Word Wizard sheet. Invite them to solve all twelve puzzles on the sheet.

- Provide an individual student with a Word Wizard sheet for a homework assignment.

- Post 1–3 Word Wizards on the bulletin board for students to solve as they come into the classroom at the start of the day.

- Add a single Word Wizard puzzle to a test, exam, homework sheet, or other printed materials that students may use during the course of the week.

- Duplicate several sheets onto oaktag or card stock (available at any office supply store). Laminate the sheets and then cut apart each of the individual puzzles. Place all the Word Wizards in a large box. Invite students to reach in at selected times during the day (after lunch or recess, after completion of seatwork, etc.) and take a puzzle to solve.

- Invite students to create their own Word Wizard puzzles to share with others in the class or with students in another room.

These puzzles provide a wealth of interesting and engaging opportunities for students to use and develop their language arts abilities. They're fun, creative, and full of high-level thinking skills.

Word Wizards 1

Name _____

Date _____

1. **T** **O** **W** **N**	2.	3. **M**　　　　　**E** GUARD **A**　　　　　**L**
4. COVER	5. chicken	6. THE CLinEAR
7. MUCH　MUCH SOON　SOON	8. WISH ★	9. Ph.D. Ph.D. Ph.D Ph.D.. Ph.D.
10. **O** **V** **A** **T** **I** **O** **N**	11. STEfrankIN	12. <u>your hat</u> keep it

Word Wizards 2

Thinking Skills
- Reorganization
- Interpretive
- Application

Name _____

Date _____

1. E K A W	2. D R A Y	3. WEAR LONG
4. WEATHER CAST CAST CAST CAST	5. C I H	6. MUCH MUCH EAT EAT
7. DINNER THE TABLE	8. FROdownNT	9. T O U C H
10. ☐ deal	11. JUST A bit MORE	12. HEAD HEELS

Word Wizards 3

Name _____

Date _____

1. S 　T 　　A 　　　R	2. MORROW MORROW	3. DARE DARE
4. FROM FLOOR CEILING CEILING	5. SHIP SHORE SHORE	6. LE VEL
7. MAN BOARD	8. NEpainCK	9. S I D E
10. CHUTE CHUTE	11. 　　　ME 　　　ME JUST ME 　　　ME	12. Peace Earth

Word Wizards 4

Name _____

Date _____

Thinking Skills
• Reorganization
• Interpretive
• Application

1. LEM ADE	2. REVO GNIDNEB	3. ☐ ing
4. D D E E R E R	5. $\frac{3}{3}$	6. SCHOOL
7. P I L F	8. VISION VISION	9. MIRlookROR
10. SS II DD EE	11. Miss Muffet	12. ONE MANY MANY

Word Wizards 5

Name _____

Date _____

1. DEFARMERLL	2. SCHOOL STAY	3. MOdriveVIE

4.
 	
KNEE
SIGN
	5.
	
	       H
	      C
	    T
	  A
	 C
		6.
		
		E

7. AGENT AGENT	8. PRICE	9. HAT

10.
 	
TURN
	11.
	  W
	    I
	      N
	        D
	          I
	            N
	              G
		12.
		
		<u>GROUND</u>
		FEET FEET
		FEET FEET
		FEET FEET

Word Wizards 6

Name _____

Date _____

1. R O R O A D S D S	2. REVO NAEL	3. GROUND GO
4. OR OR NOTHING	5. o m g y e r r	6. TOUkeepCH
7. ★ FISH	8. KEET KEET	9. WAG TRAIN
10. T O 2 P A R N	11. S T E P	12. Pig Pig Pig

Word Wizards 7

Thinking Skills
- Reorganization
- Interpretive
- Application

Name _____

Date _____

1. away	2. ONCE LIGHTLY	3. CYCLE CYCLE CYCLE
4. R E T T A B	5. **BIRD**	6. MILoneLION
7. T T R E P K P C T I	8. TALK TALK	9. K C I P TRUCK
10. PLEASE B TIME	11. ENA	12. MESNACKAL

UNIT TWO: WORD WIZARDS

Word Wizards 8

Name _____

Date _____

1. MULA MULA MULA MULA	2. Time Time	3. ✔✔ ✔ C O U N T E R
4. CHAIR	5. Lips Lips	6. <u>WHO, WHO, WHO</u> FIRST
7. <u>HOME</u> THE RANGE	8. MATION IN MATION MATION MATION	9. trouble trouble

10.   S
    L
        O
            W
	11. TREE
	PARTRIDGE
	TREE
		12. <u>WATER</u>
		THE DAM

Word Wizards 9

Name _____

Date _____

1. COorderURT	2. T I E K A M	3. Ban ana
4. HEADER HEADER	5. I'll get it it.	6. F F A A C 2 C E E
7. GO LAjumpKE	8. Score Score Score Score + 7 yrs.	9. WALK H_2O
10. key	11. pAINS	12. C-SON C-SON C-SON C-SON

UNIT TWO: WORD WIZARDS

Word Wizards 10

Name _____

Date _____

1. LEM LIME	2. OHOLENE	3. league
4. GOOD GOOD BEE BEE TRUE	5. tiJUSTme	6. E N D E N D E N D
7. SUNNY SIDE	8. MAN MAN MAN MAN	9. EVERYTHING PIZZA
10. D L O H	11. TIvalNE	12. 1. night 2. night

UNIT THREE

Analogies

When we make an analogy, we are comparing like items or concepts. Additionally, we are trying to determine the relationship between ideas. These acts help increase our level of understanding because the more interconnections we create between concepts leads to increased levels of comprehension over a wide range of disciplines.

Gifted readers benefit from analogies simply because analogies provide them with multiple opportunities to see how words "work" and multiple opportunities to create understandings. Comparing unfamiliar items to familiar items enhances comprehension. The similarity between the items is based on the relationship being compared, not the items themselves. For example, an arrow is a good analogy for a quill on a porcupine. Initially it is easier to determine relationships between related items; eventually you want to move students toward looking for similarities between unrelated items.

This unit provides you with a wide selection of analogy activities to share with your gifted students. These activities are in sequential order, with one skill building upon the other.

- **Classifications:** These initial activities encourage students to classify words into general categories. Although these are not formal analogies, they help students understand the relationships that can exist between like items.

  Example: What does this group of words have in common:
  mile   yard   inch   foot

- **Which Doesn't Belong:** Here students determine a unifying relationship between three or four listed items. They then identify the one word that does not share the feature or features of the other three.

  Example: Which does not belong with the other three?
  Flagstaff   Phoenix   Tucson   Santa Fe

- **Nonsense Groups:** A group of four words or concepts sharing a common characteristic is categorized under a nonsense term. A second group does not share the characteristic. From a third group, students select the one word or concept that could be included with those in the first group.

  Example: These are CLAMORS:
  colony   herd   pack   flock

  These are not CLAMORS:
  workers   parasite   caribou   roost

  Which of these is a CLAMOR?
  host   solitary   game   school

- **Type by Type:** In this section, students examine various types of analogous relationships. These include 1) *synonyms* vs. *antonyms,* and 2) *kind of* vs. *part of.*

  Examples: Classify the following analogy as a) synonyms or b) antonyms
  Mighty is to **strong** as **weak** is to **puny**

  Classify the following analogy as a) kind of or b) part of
  Mystery is to **novel** as **rap** is to **music**

- **Completions:** First, students must determine how two given words or concepts are related. Then, working with a third word or concept, they create another pair related to each other in the same way.

  Example: meridian : **line of longitude** :: **parallel** : _____

  Practice in analogies provides gifted students with a plethora of creative learning opportunities. The true value will be when students are afforded opportunities to create their own analogies (using these examples as models) to share with each other. Regular and frequent practice with analogies stimulates divergent thinking and fosters a deeper appreciation for language in both oral and written formats.

Classifications 1

Name _____

Date _____

Thinking Skills
- Literal
- Reorganization

Directions:

Look at each group of four words. What do they share in common?

1. caldera, cone, magma, lava	
2. slippers, shoes, socks, loafers	
3. snow, ice, sleet, dew	
4. oak, maple, birch, aspen	
5. Arizona, Colorado, New Mexico, Utah	
6. petal, flower, stem, leaf	
7. sloth, anaconda, poison dart frog, tapir	
8. eyes, ears, lips, nostrils	
9. oxygen, hydrogen, helium, carbon dioxide	
10. wood, steel, brick, cement	

Classifications 2

Name _____

Date _____

Directions:
Look at each group of four words. What do they share in common?

1. walk, skip, hop, amble	
2. fish, bird, mammal, reptile	
3. sill, pane, glass, screen	
4. ruby, crimson, scarlet, carmine	
5. park, green, square, plaza	
6. pinky, thumb, ring, forefinger	
7. talon, wing, feather, beak	
8. knife, blade, saw, ax	
9. twilight, dawn, sunrise, noon	
10. Harrisburg, Erie, Pittsburgh, Philadelphia	

Classifications 3

Thinking Skills
• Literal
• Reorganization

Name _____

Date _____

Directions:

Look at each group of four words. What do they share in common?

1. dribble, trickle, percolate, ooze	
2. hurricane, tsunami, earthquake, tornado	
3. strike, whack, sock, bat	
4. den, hive, cave, lair	
5. granite, marble, obsidian, pyrite	
6. galley, kitchen, cookroom, scullery	
7. parka, jacket, overcoat, blazer	
8. paste, glue, mucilage, cement	
9. mirthful, joyous, gleeful, merry	
10. Mohawk, Navaho, Apache, Iroquois	

Classifications 4

Name _____

Date _____

Directions:

Look at each group of four words. What do they share in common?

1. wren, ostrich, starling, peregrine	
2. avenue, freeway, highway, lane	
3. war, cool, temperate, cold	
4. careless, untidy, sloppy, messy	
5. locomotive, tender, caboose, dome	
6. sleeve, button, cuff, lapel	
7. meteor, comet, asteroid, shooting star	
8. school, herd, pride, covey	
9. tone, pitch, rhythm, tambor	
10. yelp, squawk, bellow, blat	

Which Doesn't Belong? 1

Thinking Skills
• Literal
• Reorganization

Name _____

Date _____

Directions:

Three terms or concepts in each group below have something in common. A fourth item in each group doesn't belong with the other three. Circle the unrelated term or concept.

1. Phoenix	Honolulu	Harrisburg	Chicago
2. Boulder	Colorado Springs	Santa Fe	Denver
3. Trenton	St. Louis	Salem	Baton Rouge
4. Minneapolis	Madison	Milwaukee	Green Bay
5. Oregon	Montana	North Dakota	Minnesota
6. Florida	Alabama	Georgia	Ohio
7. Maine	Missouri	New Hampshire	Vermont
8. Iowa	Illinois	Indiana	Idaho

Which Doesn't Belong? 2

Name _____

Date _____

Directions:

Three terms or concepts in each group below have something in common. A fourth item in each group doesn't belong with the other three. Circle the unrelated term or concept.

1. volcanoes	earthquakes	tsunamis	thunderstorms
2. rain forest	cape	savanna	desert
3. ranching	farming	grazing	hunting
4. solar	geothermal	nuclear	hydroelectric
5. valley	mesa	butte	plateau
6. inlet	ocean	bay	gulf
7. town	village	city	province
8. avenue	street	route	boulevard

Which Doesn't Belong? 3

Name _____

Date _____

Directions:

Three terms or concepts in each group below have something in common. A fourth item in each group doesn't belong with the other three. Circle the unrelated term or concept.

1. tongue	nose	nerve	skin
2. retina	iris	cornea	pupil
3. sweet	creamy	sour	bitter
4. dermis	hair	fingernail	epidermis
5. sponges	shark	echinoderm	mollusk
6. head	thorax	abdomen	compound eyes
7. nucleus	cytoplasm	chromosomes	cell wall
8. fir	pine	oak	spruce

Which Doesn't Belong? 4

Name _____

Date _____

Directions:

Three terms or concepts in each group below have something in common. A fourth item in each group doesn't belong with the other three. Circle the unrelated term or concept.

1. crust	soil	core	mantle
2. mountain	magma	ash	lava
3. snow	sleet	frost	rain
4. Pluto	Neptune	Earth	Uranus
5. coal	oil	natural gas	solar energy
6. shale	sandstone	limestone	slate
7. cirrus	series	cumulus	stratus
8. hurricane	typhoon	tornado	cyclone

UNIT THREE: ANALOGIES

Nonsense Groups 1

Thinking Skills
- Literal
- Reorganization

Name _____

Date _____

Directions:

Study the words in the following groups. Notice the features shared by members of the first group. Draw a circle around the word in the last group in each set that has the same feature(s) as those in the first group.

These are PERWORDS:	larch	cedar	hemlock	spruce
These are not PERWORDS:	maple	nectarine	walnut	ash
Which of these is a PERWORD?	poplar	sycamore	fir	eucalyptus

These are DISTEMS:	rust	smut	mushroom	yeast
These are not DISTEMS:	algae	moss	morel	spore
Which of these is a DISTEM?	conifer	mold	dicot	juniper

Nonsense Groups 2

Thinking Skills
- Literal
- Reorganization

Name _____

Date _____

Directions:

Study the words in the following groups. Notice the features shared by members of the first group. Draw a circle around the word in the last group in each set that has the same feature(s) as those in the first group.

These are MISTRANS:	km	mm	m	cm
These are not MISTRANS:	kg	dg	g	l
Which of these is a MISTRAN?	kl	ml	cg	dm

These are YORDITS:	foam	wood	oil	cork
These are not YORDITS:	plastic	cardboard	iron	wool
Which of these is a YORDIT?	lead	glass	ice	soil

From *Creative Activities for Gifted Readers, 3–6* © Good Year Books. This page may be reproduced for classroom use only by the actual purchaser of the book. www.goodyearbooks.com

Nonsense Groups 3

Name _____

Date _____

Directions:

Study the words in the following groups. Notice the features shared by members of the first group. Draw a circle around the word in the last group in each set that has the same feature(s) as those in the first group.

These are SINYORS:	Yellowstone	Zion	Yosemite	Everglades
These are not SINYORS:	Helena	Mojave	Duluth	Superior
Which of these is a SINYOR?	Great Salt Lake	Panhandle	Mammoth Cave	Baltimore

These are NEBRADS:	Michigan	Ontario	Erie	Superior
These are not NEBRADS:	Atlantic	Tahoe	Seneca	Okeechobee
Which of these is a NEBRAD?	Chesapeake	Iowa	Galveston	Huron

Nonsense Groups 4

Name _____

Date _____

Directions:

Study the words in the following groups. Notice the features shared by members of the first group. Draw a circle around the word in the last group in each set that has the same feature(s) as those in the first group.

These are NATRIGS:	Arctic Circle	International Date Line	Tropic of Cancer	Equator
These are not NATRIGS:	line	time zone	latitude	boundary
Which of these is a NATRIG?	longitude	Prime Meridian	parallel	South Pole

These are BUGDUGS:	gulf	channel	bay	harbor
These are not BUGDUGS:	plateau	range	canyon	hill
Which of these is a BUGDUG?	cliff	valley	highland	sound

Type by Type 1

Thinking Skill
- Interpretive

Name _____

Date _____

Directions:

Each of the analogies below is either a synonym or antonym. Synonyms are words that mean the same (**fast** is to **speedy** as **old** is to **ancient**). Antonyms are words that mean the opposite (**little** is to **big** as **short** is to **tall**). Circle the letter after each analogy that tells what type it is (S = synonym, A = antonym).

1. **tug** is to **pull** as **shove** is to **push**   S   A

2. **seaweed** is to **kelp** as **fungus** is to **mold**   S   A

3. **rest** is to **work** as **slave** is to **toil**   S   A

4. **trim** is to **prune** as **cut** is to **clip**   S   A

5. **flexible** is to **stiff** as **hard** is to **soft**   S   A

6. **beak** is to **bill** as **hoof** is to **paw**   S   A

7. **stare** is to **gaze** as **watch** is to **look**   S   A

8. **damp** is to **arid** as **humid** is to **dry**   S   A

9. **yell** is to **whisper** as **scream** is to **murmur**   S   A

10. **snake** is to **serpent** as **rat** is to **rodent**   S   A

Type by Type 2

Name _____

Date _____

Directions:

Each of the analogies below is either a synonym or antonym. Synonyms are words that mean the same (**fast** is to **speedy** as **old** is to **ancient**). Antonyms are words that mean the opposite (**little** is to **big** as **short** is to **tall**). Circle the letter after each analogy that tells what type it is (S = synonym, A = antonym).

1. **red** is to **crimson** as **brown** is to **sienna**   S   A

2. **sea** is to **ocean** as **hill** is to **mountain**   S   A

3. **considerate** is to **insulting** as **rude** is to **polite**   S   A

4. **lift** is to **raise** as **sag** is to **droop**   S   A

5. **power** is to **strength** as **vigor** is to **energy**   S   A

6. **soften** is to **melt** as **freeze** is to **harden**   S   A

7. **initiate** is to **terminate** as **mobile** is to **stationary**   S   A

8. **plethora** is to **many** as **modicum** is to **few**   S   A

9. **traverse** is to **travel** as **immobilize** is to **stop**   S   A

10. **vertical** is to **horizontal** as **latitude** is to **longitude**   S   A

Type by Type 3

Name _____

Date _____

Directions:

Each of the analogies below is either a "part of" or "kind of." In a "part of" analogy, the item named by one word is part of what is named by another word (**lettuce** is to **salad** as **wing** is to **bird**). In a "kind of" analogy, the item named by one word is similar to the item named by another word (**tennis** is to **volleyball** as **football** is to **soccer**). Circle the letters after each analogy that tell the type of analogy (PO = part of, KO = kind of).

1. **twig** is to **branch** as **finger** is to **hand**   PO   KO

2. **page** is to **book** as **book** is to **library**   PO   KO

3. **atrium** is to **house** as **gallery** is to **museum**   PO   KO

4. **raptor** is to **bird** as **constrictor** is to **reptile**   PO   KO

5. **lapel** is to **shirt** as **cuff** is to **trousers**   PO   KO

6. **nest** is to **hive** as **cave** is to **burrow**   PO   KO

7. **cambium** is to **tree** as **pistol** is to **flower**   PO   KO

8. **talon** is to **claw** as **cuticle** is to **finger**   PO   KO

9. **rap** is to **music** as **pointalism** is to **art**   PO   KO

10. **hydrogen** is to **water** as **sodium** is to **salt**   PO   KO

Type by Type 4

Name _____

Date _____

Directions:

Each of the analogies below is either a "part of" or "kind of." In a "part of" analogy, the item named by one word is part of what is named by another word (**lettuce** is to **salad** as **wing** is to **bird**). In a "kind of" analogy, the item named by one word is similar to the item named by another word (**tennis** is to **volleyball** as **football** is to **soccer**). Circle the letters after each analogy that tell the type of analogy (PO = part of, KO = kind of).

1. **graphite** is to **pencil** as **ink** is to **pen**   PO   KO

2. **legume** is to **vegetable** as **veal** is to **meat**   PO   KO

3. **puce** is to **color** as **hostel** is to **dwelling**   PO   KO

4. **flour** is to **cake** as **filling** is to **pie**   PO   KO

5. **asphalt** is to **freeway** as **gravel** is to **lane**   PO   KO

6. **moose** is to **herbivore** as **lion** is to **carnivore**   PO   KO

7. **index** is to **manual** as **harp** is to **lamp**   PO   KO

8. **ketch** is to **sailboat** as **apricot** is to **fruit**   PO   KO

9. **drawer** is to **bureau** as **cupboard** is to **kitchen**   PO   KO

10. **spine** is to **succulent** as **tentacle** is to **squid**   PO   KO

Completions 1

Name _____

Date _____

Directions:

Look at each line. Each pair of words that are separated by a single colon are related. Fill in the blank space with a word or phrase that shares the same relationship with the third word in the line.

Example:

meridian : line of longitude :: parallel : <u>line of latitude</u>

1. whale : mammal :: perch : _____

2. >32°F : dew :: _____ : frost

3. twilight : _____ :: sunrise : dawn

4. _____ : sun :: soil and rocks : moon

5. Miami : Florida :: Detroit : _____

6. tendril : bean :: _____ : corn

7. Montana : _____ :: Mississippi : Magnolia State

8. _____ : fish :: lungs : human

Completions 2

Name _____

Date _____

Directions:

Look at each line. Each pair of words that are separated by a single colon are related. Fill in the blank space with a word or phrase that shares the same relationship with the third word in the line.

Example:

meridian : line of longitude :: parallel : <u>line of latitude</u>

1. wind speed : anemometer :: earthquake : _____

2. Pacific : Oregon :: _____ : South Carolina

3. water : _____ :: wind : weathering

4. _____ : Alaska :: Olympia : Washington

5. shale : slate :: limestone : _____

6. meteorology : weather :: _____ : weather conditions

7. Washington : _____ :: Florida : oranges

8. _____ : granite :: sedimentary : sandstone

From *Creative Activities for Gifted Readers, 3–6* © Good Year Books. This page may be reproduced for classroom use only by the actual purchaser of the book. www.goodyearbooks.com

Completions 3

Name _____

Date _____

Directions:

Look at each line. Each pair of words that are separated by a single colon are related. Fill in the blank space with a word or phrase that shares the same relationship with the third word in the line.

Example:

meridian : line of longitude :: parallel : <u>line of latitude</u>

1. frog : amphibian :: snake : _____

2. Cape Horn : South America :: _____ : Africa

3. spruce: _____ :: oak : deciduous

4. _____ : masticate :: stomach : digest

5. Caribbean : Sea :: Hudson : _____

6. fuel : car :: _____ : body

7. scale : _____ :: ruler : measure

8. _____ : ant :: arachnid : spider

Completions 4

Name _____

Date _____

Directions:

Look at each line. Each pair of words that are separated by a single colon are related. Fill in the blank space with a word or phrase that shares the same relationship with the third word in the line.

Example:

meridian : line of longitude :: parallel : <u>line of latitude</u>

1. Iceland : Atlantic :: New Zealand : _____

2. 100°C : boiling point :: _____ : freezing point

3. Mariana Trench : _____ :: Mt. Everest : Nepal

4. _____ : evaporation :: gas : condensation

5. elephant : tusk :: deer : _____

6. level : seesaw :: _____ : paper cutter

7. 45° : _____ :: 90° : west

8. _____ : hydrogen :: compound : water

Activities

Gifted students need to engage in long-term learning experiences. Such opportunities will help them realize the value of reading as a lifelong skill. The activities in this unit provide a variety of multifaceted assignments, each designed as a separate lesson. With these activities, students have an opportunity to investigate an area of interest for an extended period of time, ensuring maximum involvement and investigation.

Each activity includes both thinking-skills and creative-extension assignments. Initially, you may wish to give the activities to small groups of two to four students. This strategy will provide opportunities for group members to share ideas and options appropriate to completing the activity. Later, students may want to pursue activities independently and report their discoveries to the rest of the class.

Although there are no time limits for any of these activities, each should take about one to two weeks to complete. Students may elect to do them as an extension of their regular reading program, as extra-curricular work, or as assignments to investigate outside of schoolwork.

Integrated with the regular reading curriculum, these activities provide gifted readers with a variety of offerings throughout the year. With the emphasis on self-selection, students can use and extend their reading skills in worthwhile activities that have personal significance and meaning.

Dictionary Dig

THINKING SKILLS
Literal, Reorganization

Ask each student to select a topic of interest, a favorite hobby, or an activity. Then have students look through old magazines for words, phrases, sentences, photos, and illustrations related to the subject area. Tell students to assemble these items into a specifically designed scrapbook or notebook. Afterward, these minidictionaries can be set up in various displays around the classroom.

You can vary this activity by directing students to do some research on the history and design of dictionaries. What were some of the first dictionaries, and who created them? How are words selected for dictionaries? How are dictionaries edited and updated? How many different types of dictionaries are there? This portion of the project can be a long-term activity, to include a special display or mural to which additional information can be added periodically.

CREATIVE EXTENSION
Flexibility

Have students create a special dictionary of important vocabulary words found in an individual book or reading selection. What words or definitions are necessary for someone to comprehend concepts in a selected book? Students can create their special dictionaries and display them alongside the books they accompany.

Question and Answer

THINKING SKILLS
Literal, Evaluation

Provide students with several examples of questionnaires and surveys. Direct them to examine each and to make a list of the qualities that are included in a well-designed questionnaire. Afterward, ask students to develop a questionnaire designed to obtain information about people's favorite children's books and favorite book characters. Have students work individually to interview different groups of people, both in and out of school. For example, students could survey (1) peers, (2) parents and other younger adults, and (3) grandparents and senior citizens, noting any similarities or differences between the responses of three groups. Are there any books or characters that appear on all three lists? Are certain authors more popular in specific age groups?

After students have collected their results, have them prepare a graph or chart to display the findings. You may also wish to have them make up a special report to present to other students. A display could also be created and set up in the school or public library.

CREATIVE EXTENSION
Elaboration

Have students put together a CD, DVD, videotape, or PowerPoint presentation of their results for presentation to other classes. Their production should contain the results of their survey, photos of some of the books mentioned, plot outlines, and appropriate evaluations of selected books. As they develop and analyze other questionnaires or surveys, they can include those results in subsequent presentations.

Cross Words

THINKING SKILLS
Literal, Application

Distribute several examples of crossword puzzles to individuals or small groups of students. Have them practice solving the puzzles, and then ask them to determine the characteristics that go into making a good crossword puzzle. Afterward, have students take the puzzle grid from one of the puzzles they have worked and eliminate all the clues. Direct them to use the grid to create an original crossword puzzle based on words from a popular children's book. They may wish to use character names, descriptions, settings, or events from the story to create their puzzles.

Some students may enjoy developing an original crossword puzzle from scratch. Provide students with graph paper (1" x 1") to get started and ask them to create an original puzzle based on words from a recently read story. Upon completion, these puzzles can be made available to students in other classes to solve and enjoy.

CREATIVE EXTENSION
Originality

Show students a variety of other word puzzles (acrostics, anagrams, and so on) and have small groups of pupils create some original puzzles for selected stories. To provide examples, you may want to obtain some old puzzle books (yard sales and used-book stores are good places to get them) to show to your students.

Jack Be Fleet

THINKING SKILLS
Reorganization, Interpretive

Provide students with opportunities to read several examples of familiar nursery rhymes. Afterward, direct individuals or small groups of students to rewrite selected nursery rhymes from a different point of view, such as to rewrite "Little Miss Muffett" from the spider's point of view, retell the story of Little Bo Peep from a sheep's point of view, or rewrite "Hey Diddle Diddle" from the moon's point of view. After students have completed several of these rewrites, you can post selected stories on the bulletin board for all to enjoy.

An alternative strategy would be to have students provide new endings to selected nursery rhymes. They can use colloquial language and familiar settings to alter rhymes with some humorous or unusual results. For example: "Jack be nimble, Jack be quick, Jack jumped over the candlestick, and was given a citation for having an open flame in the house." Or "Jack and Jill went up the hill to fetch a pail of water, but decided to have a picnic instead." It's not important that all lines rhyme in these creations. Rather, the emphasis should be on having fun in creating some original adaptations.

CREATIVE EXTENSION
Elaboration

Small groups of students may wish to dramatize some of their nursery rhyme "rewrites." Encourage pupils to develop a playlet based on their new creations for presentation to a younger group of students or possibly for videotaping. Students should plan some time after the presentation to discuss both the original version and their adaptation with the audience. This activity offers a wonderful opportunity for students to appreciate the various ways a piece of writing can be interpreted.

Ha Ha, Hee Hee

THINKING SKILLS
Reorganization, Evaluation

Ask students to collect various examples of humor. These could include tall tales, puns, one-liners, slapstick, shaggy dog stories, limericks, comic strips, or practical jokes. Students should use a variety of classroom, library, or home resources for their research. Afterward, have students assemble their collections into scrapbooks, with several examples used to illustrate each form. Students may also wish to include of bibliography of selected joke books available in the school library. Have pupils create individual scrapbooks or assemble a large class scrapbook to display their work. Make sure these collections are available to others in the class or school.

CREATIVE EXTENSION
Originality

Have students try their hand at writing a comic strip, joke book, or humorous skit. Ask them to research the elements that make up a humorous presentation and incorporate those elements into their efforts. Be sure to take time to discuss some of the difficulties students encounter in trying to create their own humor.

Do-It-Yourself Workbooks

THINKING SKILLS
Reorganization, Evaluation

Demonstrate the layout and format of several reading series workbooks. Then direct students to develop a list of some of the features and exercises used in workbooks. You may wish to supplement the reading series workbooks with those designed for independent work.

Afterward, ask small groups of students to develop specialized workbooks for some selected stories of children's books. Students should create appropriate exercises and activities that could be used by other students. Initially, you may wish to have students create exercises for some of their favorite books; later, they can create activities for books used by students in other grades. All of the materials and exercises could be duplicated and assembled into notebooks for student use. You may wish to notify colleagues in other grades on the availability of these student-created workbooks and have your students share them with other classes.

CREATIVE EXTENSION
Fluency

After students have had sufficient practice in creating workbooks for children's books and stories, ask them to create workbooks for other types of printed materials as well. For example, they can create workbook exercises for a newspaper, a travel brochure, a job application form, or a dictionary. The resulting workbooks could then be used for a variety of free-time activities throughout the year.

Catalog Capers

THINKING SKILLS
Reorganization, Evaluation

Have children obtain several examples of children's book catalogs. Students can get such catalogs from the school librarian or can send away for them from various publishers. When they have collected several catalogs, discuss the format and design of each. What makes one catalog more visually appealing than another? Do individual book descriptions help in deciding whether to buy a particular book?

After students have had an opportunity to look through several catalogs, ask them to create a catalog of selected books in your classroom. Direct them to develop their own classification or cataloging system. To aid in constructing the catalog, provide them with construction paper, blank paper, crayons, and markers. Allow students to use a computer with word-processing software, if possible. Ask students to decide on the illustrations and descriptions that will be needed to assist others in selecting books from the catalog. After completion, the catalog can be made a permanent part of the classroom library, with new pages included as new books are added to the room.

CREATIVE EXTENSION
Elaboration

Bring in several general merchandise catalogs (such as J. C. Penney's) and direct students to browse through them. Have pupils select items that should be in the ideal classroom. What types of merchandise or equipment would help create the perfect learning environment for students? Have pupils cut out illustrations of items and develop their own special classroom catalog. Encourage them to defend their choices.

New Labels

THINKING SKILLS
Reorganization, Appreciation

Have students bring in several examples of canned or bottled food, such as canned vegetables, salad dressings, and soups. Ask students to remove the labels from each item (the label and container can each be marked with a special code prior to removal). Direct students to list the type of information found on each label and to determine how much of the label information is important in making a buying decision about that particular product. Afterward, have each student select a product and design a brand new label for it—one that would appeal to a special group of people (for example, children, doctors, people from another country, people on a diet). What information should be included on the new label that would entice someone to purchase the product? Students can display their new labels along with the originals and evaluate the appeal factor of each. It may be necessary for students to set up an evaluation system or checklist of desirable characteristics.

CREATIVE EXTENSION
Originality

Some students may enjoy doing research on advertising. What are some good advertising techniques, and how are they used? Later, students may want to use this information to create "labels" for some books in the classroom or school library. For instance, what qualities should be listed that would encourage someone to read a certain book? Be sure to have students set up a display of selected books with their individually designed labels.

In the Cards

THINKING SKILLS
Reorganization, Appreciation

Direct students to each select a favorite story character. Have them draw an illustration of the character on the front of a piece of cardboard (or a 3" x 5" index card) and then write biographical data about the character on the reverse of the card. Students may wish to bring in baseball cards to use as examples. Once they have the idea, direct students to create a series of biographical cards for (a) an individual story; (b) a group of stories about a single character or by a selected author, or (c) all characters in a particular story.

Have students develop a classifying system to keep track of the cards as they are developed. Set up a special place in the classroom where the cards can be kept and made available to all students. Prior to reading a story or book, a student will be able to pull appropriate biographical cards from the file and consult them.

CREATIVE EXTENSION
Originality

Using the rules for a popular card game such as "Old Maid," have students develop their own game based on the characters in a favorite book or story. Give students freedom to simplify rules or create their own based on the number or kinds of characters in a story.

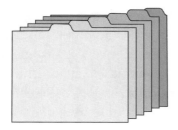

. . . By Its Cover

THINKING SKILLS
Reorganization, Appreciation

Direct students to create a series of "shape books." A shape book is made up of blank pages stapled between two sheets of oaktag and then cut into the shape of a popular object. For example, the following titles could be used for books cut into the corresponding shapes:

"All about Me" (shape of a child)
"TV Favorites" (shape of a television set)
"Baseball Stories" (shape of a baseball)
"Autumn Poems" (shape of a leaf)
"Halloween Horror" (shape of a ghost)

Once students have created a variety of shape books, ask them to write an original story inside each one.

One variation would be to have students create shape books based on individual stories read in class. Students can cut out words, pictures, or headlines from old newspapers or magazines and paste them on the pages in each shape book. The shape books could be displayed on the bulletin board or in a special file.

CREATIVE EXTENSION
Elaboration

There are many ways to create self-made books. Have students initiate some research in the library and locate three different ways of making a book. Encourage individuals to try each method and report their results. Which method is easiest? most enjoyable? Be sure students have an opportunity to display their work.

Book Games

THINKING SKILLS
Reorganization, Application

Discuss with students the qualities that go into a good table game. Have them make lists of the features they enjoy most about some of their favorite games. What qualities make for an enjoyable game?

Next, ask small groups of students to each select a favorite book and turn it into a table game. Have students bring in old or discarded board games from home. Using pieces of construction paper, markers, cardboard squares, and other materials, students can create pieces for a game based on story characters, settings, or event. Students may even wish to set up bonus cards or their own form of money to use with a game.

You can vary this activity by having two separate groups of students each develop a separate game for the same book. Another option would be to have a single group of students create a series of games based on books by a single author. Provide children with opportunities to create a variety of games for various books, and store the games in a convenient place in the classroom for all to enjoy.

CREATIVE EXTENSION
Flexibility, Originality

Have students research the history of parlor games. How were they created and why? When did they begin, and what have been some of the more popular games? Direct pupils to construct an appropriate display or mural illustrating both indoor games that were popular 200 years ago and those popular today.

Book It!

THINKING SKILLS
Reorganization, Application

Encourage students to investigate a number of library resources on making their own books. Have them create a special display on the various ways self-made books can be created.

Later, challenge students to create some specialized types of books. The following suggestions may get you started:

1. Have students do some research on the history and creation of breakfast cereals. Direct them to assemble their information in a book that uses the front and back panels of a cereal box as covers.
2. If appropriate, have students do a history of their family using a collage of family photographs for the book cover.
3. Trace and cut out a silhouette of each student. Direct students to write a brief autobiography of themselves on sheets of paper cut in the shape of their silhouette. Afterward, assemble all the silhouettes into a large class book.

Encourage students to develop additional ideas for books or book covers that incorporate shapes, designs, or components from the subjects they are writing about.

CREATIVE EXTENSION
Elaboration

Groups of students may wish to establish a bookmaking class for demonstration to other students in the school. The class can be supplemented with a student-designed pamphlet or brochure on how pupils can create their own books. The production of a videotape, CD, DVD, or PowerPoint presentation could also be a part of this activity.

Readers Wanted!

THINKING SKILLS
Reorganization, Application

Provide students with several examples of job application forms. Have them make a list of the information requested on most of the forms (name, education level, experience, and so on). Ask them whether any information requested is specific to a certain form or to a special job.

Next, ask groups of students to create a special application form for readers. Tell students that they are in charge of a children's book company and that they need to hire some readers for their books. What kind of information should a potential applicant include on an application form? What should the book company president know before hiring the best readers for the job? Direct students to work together in small groups to develop appropriate application forms. Can they develop specialized forms for special types of books (biographies, adventure stories, mysteries)?

One variation of this activity would be to have students create a special application form for potential book authors. What information would a publisher want to know about an author before "hiring" him or her to write a book, particularly a children's book?

CREATIVE EXTENSION
Elaboration

Ask students to interview a variety of adults throughout the school district (custodians, secretaries, teachers, superintendent, cafeteria workers, and so on) about their favorite books or reading material, their experiences in learning to read, or magazines they read frequently.

Have students develop biographies of selected individuals based on reading habits and experiences. These biographies can be collected into a scrapbook to be enjoyed by all.

Advertising Pays

THINKING SKILLS
Interpretive, Application

Bring several classified ads to school to share with students. Plan some time to discuss the more common abbreviations used in various ads. Provide time for students to look through the daily news-paper to select and "decode" several ads.

Next, direct students to create their own classified ad section for a selected book. For example, a "Job Wanted" ad could be created for a story character, a "Homes for Sale" ad could be developed for a character's house, or a "Cars for Sale" ad could be designed for a character's transportation. Students can work together to develop and create a variety of classified ads for a single book. They can then assemble these into a large classified section for display on the bulletin board.

Later, students may wish to create a classified ad section for a group of books by a single author or for a group of books about a single character.

CREATIVE EXTENSION
Originality

Have groups of students work with the school librarian to create classified ads for recent library purchases. Students may wish to develop, write, and "publish" a regularly issued newsletter listing some of the newest library acquisitions. The newsletter could be distributed through-out the school on a regular basis.

Answer First

THINKING SKILLS
Interpretive, Application

Using the format of the TV game show *Jeopardy!*, write a word or group of words on the chalkboard and challenge students to develop twenty original questions that would have that item as the answer. Next, give students a whole list of "answers" to provide questions for. You may wish to keep all the "answers" in a single category, such as "story characters," and have students work individually in developing their lists of questions. Here are some "answers" to get you started:

> Clifford
> The Wild Things
> Tom Sawyer
> Laura Ingalls Wilder
> Madeline
> Amelia Bedelia
> Ramona

As an additional challenge to your students, put an "answer" on the chalkboard (selected from a specific subject area) at the beginning of the day. Encourage groups of students to develop as many questions as possible by the end of the day.

CREATIVE EXTENSION
Fluency

Students may want to modify this strategy in small groups. Have one student write a list of ten questions, all of which have the same answer. Challenge other students to guess the answer within a specified time period. Later, students can generate a smaller number of questions before others determine the correct answer. Direct students to confine their questions to a single subject area.

Character Sketches

THINKING SKILLS
Interpretive, Application

Provide students with several examples of popular magazines, such as *Time, People,* and *Sports Illustrated.* Have students read several issues of each magazine to get a feel for the editorial content or slant of each. Next, have each student select a favorite storybook character and write three different biographical sketches of that character as they might appear in three different magazines. For example, how would Snow White be portrayed in *Time, People,* and *Sports Illustrated* magazines? Have students discuss the features of each character that would be emphasized in each of the respective magazines.

After students have written their individual character sketches, have them put together a mock-up collection of articles from one selected magazine (for example, *Sports Illustrated* pieces on Rip Van Winkle, Ramona, and Peter Pan). Make sure the mock-ups are displayed in a prominent place for all to enjoy.

CREATIVE EXTENSION
Flexibility

Have students make lists of fictitious article titles (dealing with story characters) that could appear in more than one popular magazine. For example: "How to Escape the Perils of Gardening" (Jack and the Beanstalk) could appear in magazines such as *People, House and Garden,* and *Discover.*

Words and Pictures

THINKING SKILLS
Interpretive, Application

Provide students with several examples of wordless picture books. Lead a discussion on how this type of literature is created and how the illustrations convey the plot of the story.

Afterward, have students work individually or in small groups to create some original dialogue or narration for selected picture books. Students may wish to write their stories or record them with a tape recorder. You may want to have students set up a special classroom display featuring a selection of picture books with their accompanying narrations.

Later, have students create their own wordless picture books to exchange with each other. Some pupils may wish to create narration for the picture books developed by their classmates. Have students share the criteria necessary for an effective wordless picture book. Some pupils may want to set up a rating scale for evaluating wordless picture books.

CREATIVE EXTENSIONS
Originality

Provide students with a selection of news photos (without captions). Ask them to select one photo and create an appropriate story to match the events or incidents depicted in the photo. Encourage students to bring in their own photos from home or to cut pictures from a magazine or newspaper to use for this activity. Some pupils may wish to turn a bulletin board into a large newspaper front page using a collection of photos and corresponding stories.

In the End . . .

THINKING SKILLS
Interpretive, Application

Provide students with stories cut from old workbooks or discarded storybooks. Before giving the stories to pupils, cut off the last two or three paragraphs of each one, and paste each story on an individual sheet of oaktag. Direct students to write a new ending for each tale. Upon completing this assignment, students may want to compare their endings with the original endings. Students may wish to attach their own endings to the original stories to create an interesting collection for others to enjoy during free reading time.

Vary this activity by cutting off the last page of old workbook stories and giving the pages to individual students. Ask them to write original stories that would lead up to those final events. Have the sheets bound together to create minibooks for others to enjoy.

CREATIVE EXTENSION
Originality

After students have completed several new stories, direct them to develop special-skills activity sheets for each story or collection of stories. What skills should be included on these activity sheets and why? Later, students may wish to exchange activity sheets and the corresponding stories.

Questions First

THINKING SKILLS
Interpretive, Application

Select a short story from an old workbook or discarded reading series book. Record the corresponding questions from a story in the series on a sheet of paper and distribute it to students (you may wish to distribute more than one copy of the questions to more than one student). Ask students to read each set of questions carefully and to develop an appropriate story containing the answers to the questions. Students may elect to tape-record their stories or write them. Afterward, have pupils compare their stories with the original stories.

Some students may wish to create their own set of original story questions. These can be duplicated and passed out to other pupils, each of whom can create an original story containing the answers to those questions. All of the stories and questions should be posted on the bulletin board and shared.

CREATIVE EXTENSION
Originality

Encourage students to discuss the qualities of good story questions. What features should story questions have, when are they appropriate to use, and what kind of information should they elicit? Afterward, direct pupils to establish their own rating scale for questions (such as 1–5 or A–F) to rate student, teacher, and text questions. Have students post their scales and use them to evaluate selected story questions used during the discussion of a reading series selection.

Time after Time

THINKING SKILLS
Evaluation, Appreciation

Lead a discussion on what a time capsule is and what types of items are normally put into one. Then have students brainstorm about the types of printed materials that should be put into a time capsule. You may want to establish some specifics for the capsule. For example, what types of materials would be put into a time capsule to be dug up twenty years from now? fifty years from now? one hundred years from now? Would the printed materials put into each capsule be the same or different? What items would be put in a capsule to be dug up by children, by adults, or by aliens from another planet? If students could put only ten (or twenty) items in each capsule, which ones would they include?

Have students construct a time capsule using plastic milk jugs or other nonbiodegradable material. Discuss potential printed items that should be placed in the capsule. Direct pupils to place several selected items in the capsule and bury it somewhere on the school grounds (you may need to secure permission). Students may wish to dig up the capsule after a specified length of time (a year, for example) and check the contents. Are there any items they would want to replace in a succeeding capsule?

CREATIVE EXTENSION
Originality

Have students make a report on one of the following topics and present it to the rest of the class: In one hundred years (a) How will reading be taught? (b) What kinds of books will kids enjoy? (c) What will libraries look like? (d) How will books be printed or published?

On the Spot

THINKING SKILLS
Evaluation, Appreciation

Provide students with opportunities to watch several TV interviews or to read interviews printed in popular magazines. Discuss with them the types of questions typically asked in these interviews and the information obtain from the interviewees. Have students develop a chart of attributes or characteristics needed by good interviewers. What distinguishes a good interviewer from a poor one?

Next direct students to select one of the situations below and write an appropriate interview:

1. An interview between a story character in a book and the book's author.
2. An interview between the student and the author of a book.
3. An interview between two characters in a book.
4. An interview between the student and a character in the book.
5. An interview between the student and a friend about a book.
6. A student interview of an author and one or more book characters.

These interviews can be posted on the bulletin board or developed into playlets for videotaping.

CREATIVE EXTENSION
Elaboration

Students may wish to set up some panel discussions based on the interviews they have written. One student can assume the role of a character, another the role of the author, and another the role of someone who has just read the book. If possible, students may wish to share these interviews with other classes.

Come to Your Senses

THINKING SKILLS
Evaluation, Appreciation

Discuss the five senses (taste, smell, hearing, touch, and sight). Ask students to create charts of words that could be listed under each of these sense categories (for example, the taste list might include *bitter, sweet,* and *sour*). Next, have each student select a favorite book or story and locate ten or more story words that could be placed in each of the sense categories. Ask students to defend their placement of selected words. For example, the word *grass* could be placed under smell, touch, or sight.

Later, students may wish to create individual sense booklets of words included in their favorite stories. These booklets could also contain pictures cut from old magazines to illustrate selected words.

CREATIVE EXTENSION
Fluency

Provide several groups of students with rolls of adding machine tape. Direct each group to create a roller box (a shoebox with a "window" cut out of the lid; a roll of adding machine tape is placed on a pencil stuck through the side, and the tape is then rolled past the window and through a slot in the bottom of the box). Have each group record on their tape a collection of sensory words heard or read during a specified time period. Challenge each group to collect as many words as possible to "show" on their roller box.

Ad Campaign

THINKING SKILLS
Evaluation, Application

Direct students to examine several different types of advertising, both print and nonprint. Have them collect as many different examples of advertising as they can. Discuss with students the qualities that go into an effective advertisement and what makes one advertisement better than another.

Divide students into small teams and ask each team to develop an ad campaign for a book or a series of books about the same character. Direct each group to design at least three different ways of advertising their selected book(s), one of which must be of the nonprint variety (filmstrip, video, slides, and so on). Upon completion, have each group decide on locations or situations in which to conduct their advertising campaigns. Have students set up some criteria by which each campaign can be evaluated and incorporate those criteria into a rating sheet. They may want to have an impartial panel of adults (other teachers, librarian, principal, reading specialist) judge each campaign using the student-created rating sheet.

CREATIVE EXTENSION
Fluency, Flexibility

Have students research various trade publications in education (such as *Horn Book* and *Book Links*) that regularly carry advertisements for children's books. Direct pupils to make lists of words or phrases that appear frequently in children's book ads. What similarities or differences do they note in the ads? What information in an advertisement would persuade them to purchase a particular book?

Our Town

THINKING SKILLS
Evaluation, Application

Have students work in groups to collect as many different types of printed material about your town as possible. Bulletins, brochures, newspapers, tickets, maps, and other printed materials relevant to your community should be collected from a variety of sites, including (but not limited to) the town hall, banks, stores, malls, the post office, the police station, and the Chamber of Commerce. After a variety of items have been collected, direct students to evaluate them in terms of their usefulness to (1) a new family moving into the area; (2) an elderly couple without children; (3) a single woman; (4) their own family; or (5) a non-English-speaking family. Encourage students to establish their own criteria for evaluating these items.

Later, have students create an all-inclusive brochure or newsletter that incorporates the best features of the printed items they collected. What information about their town should be included for the use of people currently living in the area or those who may move into the town? Students may wish to create their own flyer or a special collage. If possible, make arrangements with the local newspaper to distribute the students' flyer or have the collage displayed in the local bank or post office.

CREATIVE EXTENSION
Fluency

Have students create lists of printed material needed by each of the following individuals: (a) a construction worker, (b) a teenager looking for a job, (c) the owner of a sporting good store, (d) a homemaker with seven children, and (e) a minister. Have students post their lists in the classroom.

All the News

THINKING SKILLS
Evaluation, Application

Provide groups of students with copies of several popular children's books, and have each group develop a complete newspaper account of the book. For example, have one student in each group work on developing a "front page," writing up certain story events and giving them appropriate headlines (which events would be the most important to treat as front-page news?). Another student in each group can be assigned the task of selecting several events from a story that would be include on a fashion page (how were some of the characters in the book dressed?). If illustrations are not provided, can some original ones be drawn? Other students can work on developing selected story events into other newspaper sections, such as Arts & Leisure, Home and Garden, Sports, Local News, Travel, and the like.

After the students have drafted their articles, have them assemble their work into a newspaper. Duplicate the newspaper for each book and distribute it to other students or other classes. The newspapers can also be made available in the library as an enticement for others to read the "newsworthy" books.

CREATIVE EXTENSION
Flexibility

Direct students to go to the public library and find newspapers from different parts of the country. Ask them to look up a single news item and see how it is reported in each of four different newspapers. What similarities or differences do they note?

Projects

Exploring a topic in detail should be an important part of each gifted student's development as a reader. Using a variety of reading skills, a host of reference materials, and a number of reporting formats encourages students to examine given topics from a variety of directions. In addition, extended projects help students develop an appreciation for their own literacy development.

The projects in this section are designed as long-term investigations for individuals or small groups. Each one focuses on a general area of discovery and stimulates the practical application of each of the six major thinking skills and at least two creative extensions. Although no time limit has been established for these projects, each should require several weeks or months, depending on several factors: the amount of class time available each day, whether the projects are used exclusively as schoolwork or are extended into the

home or community, class make-up (gifted class versus regular heterogeneous class), and the nature and variety of resource materials available.

Before assigning any project, take time to discuss each subsection thoroughly. Students should understand the nature of each subsection, how the information can be gathered or developed, and some possible reporting formats. Initially, you may wish to have students or groups report their discoveries separately for each subsection. Later, students can use a reporting format that includes all subsections of a project.

These projects are appropriate for use throughout the school year. They are practical as long-term investigations that extend and refine necessary reading skills. With them, gifted students can learn to use their cognitive and creative abilities in meaningful "real-world" applications.

Books, Books, Books

THINKING SKILLS

Literal

List the steps in publishing or printing a book commercially.

Reorganization

Compare printing techniques in the 1700s or 1800s with the more modern methods used today. Include costs, time, number of workers needed, and so on.

Interpretive

Design, illustrate, and create a self-made book. Check out some library books on how to make your own book. Be sure to include an original story in your book.

Evaluation

Design and set up a rating system for evaluating children's books. What qualities should a good children's book have?

Appreciation

Write critiques/review of three children's books written by different authors. Prepare these reviews for possible publication in the local newspaper. What makes these books outstanding or unacceptable?

Application

Survey people in three different age groups (grandparents, parents, classmates) to determine their favorite children's books. What books are mentioned most and why? What are some of the "classics"? Record and report your results.

CREATIVE EXTENSIONS

Fluency

1. Make a list of (a) all the things you couldn't do if books were to vanish off the face of the Earth; (b) ways to compile and record information other than in books; (c) the ten best places to read a book; and (d) the five best books you have ever read.

Flexibility

2. Write a report comparing books and computers. What are the similarities? What are the differences?

Fabulous Folklore

THINKING SKILLS

Literal
Compile a booklet listing several American folktales. Include as many sources as possible.

Reorganization
Compile a list of characters from American folktales and their foreign folktale counterparts.

Interpretive
Read several Aesop's fables to some of your classmates. Encourage them to figure out the moral for each one.

Evaluation
Compare folktales that contain animals with human qualities to folktales without animals. Which type is more interesting? Which type is more effective in getting a message across?

Appreciation
Master the dialect from an Uncle Remus story and read it to the class. Do the same for a folktale from another country.

Application
Investigate several folktales and analyze them in terms of the type of ending they have (happy versus unhappy; resolved versus unresolved).

CREATIVE EXTENSIONS

Fluency
1. Place a world map on the bulletin board. On individual index cards write the titles of twenty to thirty folktales, and pin the cards around the map. Cut lengths of yarn and use each one to connect the country of origin to the card for each tale (pin one end of the yard to the card and the other end to the appropriate location on the map).

Elaboration, Originality
2. Write an original tall tale and illustrate it with a "bigger than life" mural to hang on a door or wall.

Pet Parade

THINKING SKILLS

Literal
Make a list of the five most popular breeds of dogs and the five most popular breeds of cat in this country.

Reorganization
What are some of the most popular types of pets in England? How do English tastes in pets compare with the choices of pets in this country?

Interpretive
Write a story from a pet's point of view. What does the pet see during one day? What does it think about? What kinds of things does it like to do?

Evaluation
Survey other students and adults at school about their attitudes toward owning a pet. What are the benefits? What are the drawbacks?

Appreciation
Several organizations provide pets to patients in nursing homes and to people in prisons. Why is this done? What are the results?

Application
Investigate the history, background, and mission of organizations such as the Humane Society and the ASPCA. How did they come into existence, and why do they still exist? Write a letter to your local newspaper telling the community why it should continue to support these organizations.

CREATIVE EXPRESSIONS

Originality
1. Write a story about the perfect pet. What would it look like? How would it behave? Where would it live? What would it eat? Would your perfect pet be for the whole family or just for you? Why?

Flexibility, Originality
2. Make a mural illustrating some of the similarities and differences between house cats and big cats. Use both pictures and words, and include as many different examples as possible.

Comic Relief

THINKING SKILLS

Literal
Research the history of comic strips. When was the first strip created and who wrote and drew it?

Reorganization
Compare comic strips of fifty years ago with those in today's newspapers. What differences or similarities do you note?

Interpretive
Dramatize your favorite comic strip. You may wish to create a puppet show or your own original play.

Evaluation
What are the qualities that make a comic strip enjoyable? Do all comic strips have to be funny to be good?

Appreciation
Write critiques of two popular comic strips that have been around for many years. Locate examples of those strips from ten years ago and twenty years ago. Do your critiques still apply? Why or why not?

Application
Write your own comic strip using class-mates or family members as some of the characters. Show your strip to other students and adults and record their reactions. What are some of the positive comments? negative comments?

CREATIVE EXTENSIONS

Fluency, Flexibility
1. Create four scrapbooks, each illustrating a different type of comic strip (such as humor, adventure, romance, and information). Collect several examples for each category and paste them into the appropriate scrapbook. What are some of the similarities and some of the differences between these categories of comic strips?

Elaboration
2. Most comic strips are published by syndicates. Obtain the addresses of some syndicates and write to them. Ask about the qualities they look for before they decide to publish a comic strip. You may also want to ask about some of the production techniques that are used. Ask them to send you any information or literature about their organization.

Language Lovers

THINKING SKILLS

Literal

Make a list of ten languages spoken throughout the world (each must be spoken in more than one country). Rank order them from most common (the one spoken by the most people) to least common.

Reorganization

Compare different forms of English, such as Old English versus modern English. Make a chart illustrating common words or phrases for each form.

Interpretive

Ask several students and adults to list favorite slang expressions. Record and count the results. What similarities or differences do you note between the slang expressions of adults and children? Create two dictionaries, one for kids to decipher adult language and one for adults to decipher kids' language.

Evaluation

Many businesses and governments in other countries recommend that their employees know how to read, speak, or write English. Why do you think this would be important?

Appreciation

Invent a nonverbal language (pantomime, signing). Teach your new language to a friend. What difficulties do you encounter in trying to communicate using your new language? What types of words or thoughts are you unable to convert into your language?

Application

Obtain a children's book written in a foreign language, such as Spanish or French. Try to translate it based on the illustrations and the similarity of some words to English words. Talk to a language teacher at the local high school to find out how accurate your translation is.

CREATIVE EXTENSIONS

Flexibility, Elaboration

1. There are many words in the English language that originated in other countries (for example, *curfew* came from France, and *rodeo* came from Mexico). Create a dictionary of words from other languages that have become English words, and report your findings to the class.

Fluency, Flexibility

2. Many words and phrases are specific to certain occupations, hobbies, or technologies. For example, computer talk includes such words as *CD, hard drive, modem,* and *pixels.* Make a poster listing four selected occupations and the terminology used by people working in those fields. Are there words common to more than one occupation? Are there words specific to only one field?

Food Fare

THINKING SKILLS

Literal

Look up the four basic food groups. List five examples of food for each group.

Reorganization

Compare the meals served at school with those you eat at home. What types of foods are normally served at each location? Which ones are most nutritious? most enjoyable?

Interpretive

Survey your friends on the types of foods they eat at lunch during the week, including weekends. Make a graph of your findings and send it to the principal or cafeteria manager.

Evaluation

Why is it important for people to eat a balanced diet? What are the consequences of not eating a balanced diet? Share an example from a recent news story.

Appreciation

Work with your parents to plan a weekly menu for the entire family. Write a plan for each meal, making sure all four food groups are included.

Application

Talk to the school cafeteria manager. Investigate the steps needed to plan nutritious meals for all students in the school.

CREATIVE EXTENSIONS

Fluency, Elaboration

1. Make a list of all the foods you normally eat during the week that contain sugar. Make another list of those foods that contain salt. Are there foods you normally eat that have neither sugar nor salt? Make up a menu plan for one day using foods from all four food groups that have neither sugar nor salt. Write to local colleges or government agencies for brochures or information on the hazards of too much salt or sugar in your diet.

Originality

2. What do you think food will look or taste like one hundred years from now? How will it be packaged? How will it be sold? Write a story about your ideas. Be sure to include illustrations.

Crazy Computers

THINKING SKILLS

Literal

Identify some of the earliest examples of computers and the people who invented them.

Reorganization

Compare the very first electronic computer with some of the more popular models today. What differences are there in terms of size, speed, and cost?

Interpretive

What has been the role of computers in schools? in business? What are some of the similarities between business and school applications? What are some of the differences? Survey your classmates and adults outside of school and include their ideas in your report.

Evaluation

Select several educational computer programs. Use each one yourself or obtain reviews of each program from various computer magazines. Which programs have the greatest educational value? As a potential user, what criteria are important to you in deciding on a particular program?

Appreciation

What do you think you would need to know to explain computers to an adult who has never used one? Develop a guidebook for kids to use in explaining computers to their parents.

Application

Talk to several adults and write a report on some of the changes that have come about in our world since the introduction of computers. Do adults feel that our lives are better or worse because of computers? Chart or graph some of your findings.

CREATIVE EXTENSIONS

Fluency, Elaboration

1. Make a list of the features a computer should have before a school decides to purchase one. If you could design the perfect computer for your school, what features would you want it to have? Provide some illustrations of your perfect computer.

Originality

2. What will be the role of computers in the home in twenty years? in fifty years? Make some predictions on what you would like to have computers do in your home in the future.

Sports Report

THINKING SKILLS

Literal

Make a list of the most popular participatory sports in the United States. Make another list of the most popular spectator sports. Are there any sports that appear on both lists?

Reorganization

What were some of the earliest sports in this country? in Europe? in Latin America? How do they compare with sports commonly played today?

Interpretive

Develop and produce a mock radio broadcast of a well-known sporting event. Be sure to include a pregame show, interviews, and a play-by-play description of the event.

Evaluation

Look through several sports books in the school library and compile a list of some of the greatest sports moments of all time. What factors will help you decide on the most memorable events?

Appreciation

Some high schools across the country are cutting out portions of their sports programs for a variety of reasons. What do you feel are the advantages and disadvantages of a reduced sports program at the high school level? Present your findings and opinions to some administrators in your school or district.

Application

Conduct some research in the library and investigate all the career opportunities in the field of sports. Besides players, what other occupations are connected with the world of sports? Which ones would interest you the most? Design a chart of your findings to post on the bulletin board.

CREATIVE EXTENSIONS

Originality

1. What would be the perfect sport to watch? What would be the perfect sport to participate in? Put on your thinking cap and design your own sport, game, or physical activity for each of these two categories. Provide information on the rules, number of players, timing, equipment, and other conditions.

Fluency, Originality

2. Write a report on the advantages of regular physical exercise for everyone. Make some predictions of what would happen if no one ever exercised.

Name Game

THINKING SKILLS

Literal

Make a list of the ten most common boys' names and the ten most common girls' names.

Reorganization

People's first names come from many sources. Make a chart of your classmates' names and try to discover the origin, derivation, or etymology of as many as you can.

Interpretive

Many last names or parts of last names have special meanings. Make a list of some of the more common last names along with their "translations." For example, *Miller* used to mean someone who ground wheat (at a mill). Can you interpret some of your classmates' last names?

Evaluation

Why do you think people often judge others solely on the basis of their first or last name? What would you think about someone named *Butch?* someone named *Gertude?* Make a report on how people often prejudge others on the basis of their name alone.

Appreciation

Many of the words we use today originally came from a person's name. Examples include *chauvinist, sandwich,* and *watt.* How would you feel if your name were made part of the English language? Invent a definition for your name and give two examples of how it might be used.

Application

Several organizations work in the area of etymology. Write to some of them and inquire about the techniques or procedures they use to investigate the origins of family names. Make a mural or poster illustrating your findings.

CREATIVE EXTENSIONS

Flexibility, Elaboration

1. Put a world map on the bulletin board. On separate index cards write the names of classmates, teachers, secretaries, cafeteria workers, and custodians. Use lengths of yarn to connect each card to the country of origin for each name.

Originality, Elaboration

2. Invent nicknames for some of your classmates that highlight their personalities (for example, "Happy" Johnston, "Earnest" Smith). Be sure to focus on the positive qualities of each person.

Monsters and Creatures

THINKING SKILLS

Literal

Make a list of ten creatures or monsters from folklore. Make another list of ten monsters that have appeared in movies or on television.

Reorganization

Describe some of the creatures that are popular in this country. How do they compare with creatures associated with other countries?

Interpretive

Hypothesize what would happen if Big Foot or some other creature were captured near your town. Write a short play dramatizing the events.

Evaluation

What do you feel are the characteristics that make one monster or creature scarier than another? Make up a guide that rates monsters according to how scary you think they are. Show it to some classmates to get their opinion.

Appreciation

There are several groups and organizations that investigate and collect information on creatures that are thought to exist today, such as the Loch Ness Monster and the Abominable Snowman. Write for information from one of these groups and present a report on the activities of the organization.

Application

Many people believe that several strange creatures are alive today (for example, Big Foot, Yeti, the Lock Ness Monster). Choose one of these creatures and investigate its history, background, and sightings. What scientific data are there that the creature actually exists? Make a report including illustrations, to the rest of the class.

CREATIVE EXTENSIONS

Originality

1. If you were allowed to create your own monster, what would it look like, how would it behave, where would you keep it, what would it eat, and what would it do for you? Write a story about your perfect monster. You may also wish to create your perfect monster out of clay or papier-mâché for a special display.

Flexibility, Originality

2. Design a poster on the theme of "The Most Famous Creatures of All Time." Use both illustrations and words to describe the selected creatures, and provide as many different examples as possible.

Bicycle Bonanza

THINKING SKILLS

Literal

Make a list of the major parts and components of a typical bicycle. Draw a bicycle and label all the parts.

Reorganization

There are many different types of bicycles—road bikes, racing bikes, mountain bikes, tandem bikes, and so on. Choose any two and write a report that compares their various features.

Interpretive

Set up a special exhibit in the classroom on both the history and future of bicycles. What information do you think should be featured in your exhibit?

Evaluation

How does a bicycle rank as an efficient form of transportation? How does it compare with other modes of transportation in terms of cost, maintenance, speed, durability, and design? Survey several people in school to get their reactions, and write a report on your findings.

Appreciation

Select one model of a particular brand of bicycle. Talk to people who own one as well as to salespeople in a bicycle store. Write to the manufacturer for a brochure on your chosen model. Afterward, put together a complete review of the bike that might appear in a biking magazine (you may want to look at reviews of other bikes first).

Application

Analyze the various ways bicycles are used today. Investigate the bicycle's use in exercise, transportation, communication, and sports. Look into its uses for business as well as for pleasure. Prepare a formal report to share with others in the class.

CREATIVE EXTENSIONS

Fluency, Originality

1. If you could put together a bicycle that would have everything you ever wanted on it, what would it look like? What would be its most important features? How much should it cost? How would it be used? Set up a bulletin board display to illustrate your perfect bike.

Originality, Elaboration

2. Look at several uses of a bicycling magazine and analyze the different features, articles, columns, and advertisements that normally appear within its pages. Then develop your own bike magazine to include reviews of friends' bikes, advertisements for necessary equipment, an editorial on bike safety, or other pertinent features. Assemble your "magazine" into a three-ring binder to share with others.

UNIT SIX

Story Energizers

Providing gifted students with opportunities to use both thinking and creative skills in a variety of classroom reading assignments can be an important part of their literacy development. The purpose of the worksheets, activities, and projects in this book is to stimulate an active relationship with all printed material, including regular reading series assignments. In developing this active relationship, gifted youngsters begin to value their participation in all aspects of the reading process, enlarging their reading horizons far beyond the classroom walls.

This unit provides you with a selection of thinking-skills assignments and creative extensions appropriate for any story or book. Organized into three sections—Characters, Settings, and Events—these story energizers can be used to supplement the regularly scheduled reading program. For each section there is a selection of thinking-skills questions that can be asked during the study of a selected story. You may wish to encourage students to pose these questions to each other—an option that also stimulates the generation of additional questions (which can be recorded for later use). The thinking-skills sections also include brief assignments, such as compiling lists. The creative extensions provide selected assignments designed to foster the development of all areas of creative expression.

All the story energizers only scratch the surface of possibilities; students should be encouraged to develop and design their own assignments in keeping with the specifics of individual stories.

Characters

THINKING SKILLS

Literal

1. Make a list of six words that describe the main character.

2. What were some of the problems or situations the character(s) encountered?

3. Name two events that portray the main character's personality.

4. Name all the characters. List one descriptive word for each.

Reorganization

1. Choose any character. What type of individual is that person/animal/thing?

2. List the characteristics necessary for you to like someone. How do they apply to the story character?

3. List and describe each of the major characters.

4. Rank order the story characters from most like to least liked.

Interpretive

1. Which character(s) could be eliminated from the story? Why?

2. How does the main character stand out from the other characters?

3. Do you think your friends would enjoy meeting the main character? Why?

Evaluation

1. If you had been one of the characters, would you have done anything differently? Why?

2. If you could change the behavior of any character, which one would you change? Why?

3. How do you think the main character would like your friends?

4. Compare the main character's personality at the beginning of the story with his or her personality at the end of the story.

Appreciation

1. What were some of the characteristics of the main character that you liked? Which characteristics did you dislike?

2. Would you want to read other books about these characters? Why?

3. Would you like to have one of the characters as a friend? Which one? Why?

4. How would your friends react to the characters in this story?

Application

1. What factors are important in choosing a friend?

2. What are some personality characteristics that you dislike?

3. What would you do if one or more of the characters moved into your neighborhood?

4. Did you learn anything from the main character that would be useful or harmful in your own life?

UNIT SIX: STORY ENERGIZERS

CREATIVE EXTENSIONS

Fluency

1. Make a list of all the characters might say if they came into your classroom.

2. Make a list of classmates who share personality features with one or more characters.

3. Start a collection of items (coins, artifacts, and so on) the main character might have. Construct an appropriate display.

4. Make a costume that the main character might wear. Use old clothes or scraps of material.

Flexibility

1. Illustrate some of the similarities between two or more characters. Construct a poster with appropriate designs.

2. Cut out pictures of several people from old magazines. Using a combination of body types, faces, and so on, construct a character similar to one in the story.

3. Rewrite a portion of this story with one or more of your friends as the major character(s).

4. Make a three-dimensional model of one of the characters in the story. Use clay, papier-mâché , or another appropriate medium.

Originality

1. Make a sock puppet or stick figure of the main character and act out a portion of the story.

2. Make a cartoon strip using some of the characters from the story.

3. Make a dictionary of descriptive words that could be used for each of the characters. Use words and phrases cut out of old magazines.

4. Cut out a cartoon strip from the Sunday newspaper. Erase the dialogue in the "balloons" and replace it with appropriate dialogue from the story.

Elaboration

1. If you were the author of the story, in what further episodes, events, or discoveries would you have the characters participate?

2. Develop a radio show using some of the characters from the story. You may want to listen to old-time radio shows ("The Green Hornet," "Amos and Andy," and so on) and then develop your own.

3. Write a letter to the author of the story from the viewpoint of one of the characters. What would that character want to say to the author? Would the character feel that he or she was well treated in the story?

Settings

THINKING SKILLS

Literal

1. List all the places where the story occurred.
2. Make a list of six words that describe a setting from the story.
3. Locate the probable location for the story on a map.

Reorganization

1. Draw a map of all the places mentioned in the story.
2. Select and read another story by a different author that takes place in similar surroundings.
3. Compare the settings of this story with (a) your school, (b) your town, or (c) your neighborhood.
4. Illustrate the story location.

Interpretive

1. Why did the author place the story in the location he or she did?
2. Do you feel the setting for this story was real or imaginary? Why?
3. Do you think the story could have taken place in another location? If so, where?

Evaluation

1. Why was the story setting the most appropriate place for this story to occur?
2. Could this story have taken place in your school? your neighborhood? your city? Why or why not?
3. Do you think the author would enjoy writing a story that took place in your hometown? Why?
4. Was the location of the story believable?

Appreciation

1. Would you want to live in a place similar to the story location?
2. How do you think your parents or friends would react to living in the story setting?
3. Was the author realistic in portraying the location of the story?
4. Describe the setting by writing an original poem.

Application

1. What would you do if your parents decided to move to a place similar to the location of this story?
2. What are some of the important things to consider in selecting a place to live?
3. Survey your friends on places they would like to live. Would any of them want to live in a location similar to the story setting?

CREATIVE EXTENSIONS

Fluency

1. Make a list of six other possible locations for this story.

2. Develop a list of ten descriptive phrases used in the story. After each write the name of a place or town near you that the phrase describes.

3. List all the places in the story that have (a) plants, (b) places to live, (c) electricity, and (d) animals.

4. Take photos of places in your neighborhood similar to those mentioned in the story.

Flexibility

1. Construct a chart listing story locations, important sites in your hometown, and places you have visited. What similarities do you note?

2. Cut out twenty to twenty-five pictures from old magazines or newspapers and construct a scrapbook. Under each picture list a setting from the story and identify it as similar to or different from that portrayed in the picture.

3. Select an illustration from the story and describe how it would feel to live in that setting. Write a letter to a friend explaining what you like or dislike about the setting.

Originality

1. Paint a mural of the scenes in the story. Display it on the bulletin board.

2. Make a diorama of a major setting in the story. Use a shoe box and cardboard figures.

3. Create an advertisement (radio or magazine) for the setting of the book. Induce others to buy property there.

Elaboration

1. Write a continuation of this story with your neighborhood, town, or city as the setting.

2. Plan a trip to the setting of this story. How will you get there, what will you take, and how will you survive? Make a diary of your first week there.

3. Design a travel brochure about the setting of the story. Take photos or draw original illustrations and provide appropriate captions.

Events

THINKING SKILLS

Literal

1. What were some of the most important events in the story? the least important?
2. List six story events in the correct order.
3. Summarize the story in twenty-five words or fewer.

Reorganization

1. List the characteristics of a good story. Which ones apply to this story?
2. Report the series of event that lead up to the most exciting part of the story.
3. What were the two most important events in the story?
4. Make a time line of the story events.

Interpretive

1. Why did the story end the way it did? What changes would you like to make in the ending?
2. Why did the author write this story?
3. Why would you like or dislike participating in the events of this story?

Evaluation

1. How do you think the following people would react to this story: (a) your parents; (b) your next door neighbor; (c) your brother or sister; (d) your doctor. Write an explanation for your answers.

2. Did you enjoy the way the story began? Why or why not?
3. How did the title compare with the events in the story? Was it appropriate? Why or why not?
4. Was this a believable story?

Appreciation

1. Would an older child enjoy this story? a younger child?
2. Why do you think the author chose to write the story in this manner?
3. Read another story by the same author. Are the events similar? If so, why? If not, why?
4. Do you think the topic of this story is important?
5. Explain what the title means?

Application

1. Compare the events of this story to some events in your own life. How are they similar? How are they different?
2. What would be important for an author to remember when trying to write an interesting story?
3. Do you think there is a lesson to be learned from this story? Why or why not?
4. Did you learn anything new by reading this story?

CREATIVE EXTENSIONS

Fluency

1. Make a list of twenty words that tell something about the story. Afterward, make a corresponding list of twenty synonyms, one for each word on the first list.

2. Tape-record (from TV or radio) selected events that could take place within the context of this story.

3. Stick a small branch in a coffee can filled with sand. On each twig tie a small card that illustrates or describes an important story event.

Flexibility

1. Cut out headlines from the newspaper that could be used to describe or identify events in the story. Assemble them into a scrapbook.

2. Locate another story (by a different author) that has events similar to those in this story. Write a report about some of the similarities.

3. Write a newspaper account of the story that would be enjoyed by:
   (a) a young child in another country;
   (b) your 107-year-old grandmother;
   (c) a person lost on a desert island.

Originality

1. Make a "roll movie" of several events in the story. Using a long strip of adding machine tape, draw a series of important events. Roll the strip onto a pencil and show it to a friend.

2. Dramatize the story in a play or skit.

3. Write an original song (using a popular tune) for the story events.

4. Create a crossword puzzle based on the story.

Elaboration

1. Develop a pantomime about the events in the story. Draft a continuation of the story and share it through pantomime.

2. Create a wordless picture book that illustrates the important events of the story. Create an original cover, too.

3. Create a reference guide for the story. Combine the elements of a dictionary, thesaurus, atlas, biographical dictionary, *Who's Who*, and an almanac into a booklet that would help others understand or appreciate the story.

Answer Key

Puzzles and Problems

Color My World

red tape .... complicated official routine

golden rule .... treat others as you would have them treat you

yellowjacket .... stinging insect

blacktop .... highway or road covering

blue chip .... high-quality stock

silver lining .... the good part of a bad situation

yellow streak .... cowardice

white elephant .... a useless possession

red alert .... high-priority emergency

blackmail .... obtaining payment on the basis of threats

silversmith .... one who works with silver

blue bloods .... members of socially prominent families

whitewash .... to cover up

black belt .... highest rank in tae kwon do

greenhouse .... place where plants are grown

Goldilocks .... girl who visited the three bears

red hot .... heated to a very high temperature

green thumb .... something an expert gardener is said to have

gray matter .... the brain

greenhorn .... a novice

yellow fever .... a tropical disease

blue pencil .... to edit a manuscript

blue .... to be sad

bluegrass .... special grass in Kentucky

Begin and End

Answers will vary.

Word Whip

Farm Animals	Zoo Animals
chicken	giraffe
rooster	crocodile
lamb	camel
cow	lion
horse	monkey
goose	bear
pig	llama
duck	zebra
dog	hippo

Animals Inside

Answers will vary.

Mixed-up Words

seat–eats	net–ten
read–dear	meal–lame
robe–bore	span–pans
reed–deer	part–trap
spin–nips	words–sword
coast–coats	bear–bare
rat–tar	grab–brag
oars–soar	steam–meats
mate–tame	trap–part
keep–peek	lane–lean
star–rats	pear–reap
spray–prays	lap–pal

In the Right Order

Answers will vary.

Animal Farm

An army of caterpillars
A nide of pheasants
A bob of seals
An ostentation of peacocks
A crash of rhinos
A pod of whales
A drift of hogs
A quiver of cobras
An earth of foxes
A rhumba of rattlesnakes
A family of otters
A smack of jellyfish
A glint of goldfish
A tower of giraffes
A hatch of flies
An ugly of walruses
An intrusion of cockroaches
A volery of birds
A jug of quail
A wisp of eels
A knot of toads
An exaltation of larks
A lounge of lizards
A yoke of oxen
A murder of crows
A zeal of zebras

tigers–ambush
turtles–bale
worms–clew
woodpeckers–descent
bees–erst
piglets–farrow
geese–wedge
penguins–waddle

One More Time

1. Person's name beginning with the last letter in the previous name
2. Words are in reverse alphabetical order
3. Five-letter word beginning with *I*
4. Five-letter word beginning with *Q*
5. Word that can be made from the letters in *stare*

Puzzle Me

Answers will vary.

Add One More

Answers will vary.

Crazy Headlines

1. Jack Be Nimble, Jack Be Quick
2. Old King Cole
3. Little Boy Blue
4. Georgie Porgie, Pudding and Pie
5. Ring around the Mulberry Bush
6. The Cat and the Fiddle
7. Hickory Dickory Dock
8. Humpty Dumpty
9. It's Raining, It's Pouring
10. Jack and Jill
11. Little Bo-Peep
12. Little Jack Horner
13. London Bridge Is Falling Down
14. Little Miss Muffett
15. Mary Had a Little Lamb
16. Old Mother Hubbard
17. Pat-a-Cake

A Man, a Plan, a Canal: Panama!

Answers will vary.

Up, Down, and Across

James and the Giant Peach
A Wrinkle in Time
Where the Red Fern Grows
Harry Potter and the Chamber of Secrets

Your Order, Please I

1. 3
   blank
   1
   2
   4

2. 4
   blank
   1
   3
   2

3. 2
   1
   3
   blank
   4

Pyramid Sentences

Answers will vary.

Sentence Challenge I

Answers will vary.

Answer First

Answers will vary.

What's Right? I

All plants need food.
Living things are composed of cells.
A pulley is used to pull a load.
Magma comes from the Earth's crust.
Clouds form when warm, moist air cools.

In Short

1. taxicab
2. hamburger
3. automobile
4. examination
5. bicycle
6. airplane
7. gasoline
8. veterinarian
9. submarine
10. mathematics
11. referee
12. champion

Your Order, Please II

1. 2
   blank
   3
   1
   4

2. 4
   blank
   2
   1
   3

3. 4
   3
   1
   blank
   2

The Right Size

1. seed, nail, mouse, house
2. dime, toaster, tire, elephant
3. worm, apple, lantern, hill
4. speck, light bulb, desk, elevator
5. cup, blanket, automobile, circus
6. pencil, book, table, school
7. doughnut, shoe, tuba, elm
8. bee, bird, folder, donkey

1. river, octopus, sock, ant
2. robot, squirrel, potato, pearl
3. train, aunt, record, envelope
4. bridge, chair, jacket, necklace
5. city, mayor, wagon, menu
6. porcupine, dictionary, pocket, finger
7. gym, shark, postcard, staple
8. forest, calendar, carnation, key

Sentence Challenge II

Answers will vary.

Fantastic Food

1. B, C, D, E, H
2. B, C, D, E, F, G8
3. A, B, E, H
4. A, H
5. A, B, H
6. B, C, F, G
7. B, C, D, H
8. I
9. B, C, D, E
10. A, H
11. B, C, D, E, F, H
12. D, I
13. A, B, H
14. A, B, E, H
15. A, B, H
16. B, G
17. B, C, D, E, H
18. E
19. B, C, F, G
20. A, B, H

ANSWER KEY

What's Right? II

Hawaii is farther south than Florida.
Eight states border Missouri.
NE is the opposite of SW.
One mile = 1,760 yards.
Australia and Argentina are in the
  Southern Hemisphere.

By Ones and Twos

fivek—fork—threek
threeword—toward—oneward
fivetune—fortune—threetune
elevennis—tennis—nineis
twoderful—wonderful—zeroderful
crenine—create—creseven
elevension—tension—ninesion
grnine—great—grseven
lniner—later—lsevener
Califivenia—California—Calithreenia
Elevennessee—Tennessee—Ninenessee
tomnineo—tomato—tomseveno

1. Today I'm going to the store for a crate
   of apples.
2. Once upon a time, two pirates buried
   a fortune of pieces of eight.
3. Tuesday was wonderful, except I was
   late for my foreign language class.
4. I wonder if the tutor will forget the
   fifteen books about the sixties and
   seventies.

Construction Junction

Answers will vary.

The Right Place

Drink It	**Wear It**
fluid	kimono
nectar	sandal
julep	epaulet
cola	snood
seltzer	lace
libation	serape
cordial	ornament

Ride It	**Plant It**
monorail	fern
pachyderm	legume
surrey	yam
coach	lentil
ark	conifer
blimp	sapling
equine	orchid
trapeze	
locomotive	

Front and Back

Answers will vary.

Making Cents

A = 1¢, B = 2¢, C = 3¢, etc.

Who Said That?

1. Big Bad Wolf
2. Red Riding Hood's Wolf
3. Little Miss Muffett
4. Cinderella
5. The Little Engine That Could
6. The Ugly Duckling
7. Sleeping Beauty
8. Peter Pan
9. Peter Rabbit
10. Bambi

Simile Swing

Answers will vary.

What's That?

1. Twinkle, twinkle, little star
2. Birds of a feather flock together.
3. Look before you leap.
4. Don't cry over spilt milk.
5. The pen is mightier than the sword.
6. You can't teach an old dog new tricks.
7. Spare the rod and spoil the child.
8. Where there's smoke, there's fire.
9. Too many cooks spoil the soup.
10. Dead men tell no tales.

What's in a Name?

1. I. M. Sadd
2. S. Lois Molassis
3. Page Turner
4. Ima Sparrow
5. C. Howie Runns
6. C. U. Later
7. Willie Makeit
8. Noah Lott
9. Ima Hogg
10. Jack O'Diamonds
11. Newell Leans
12. N. Struckter
13. Pat E. Kaike
14. E. Z. Duzitt

More Than One

Bat: animal, stick
Coat: clothing, cover
Horn: instrument, animal part
Slip: trip, clothing
Roll: bread, rock
Trip: fall, journey
Foot: body part, bottom
Bark: dog sound, tree part
Ring: jewelry, sound
Pen: enclosure, writing tool

Spring
band
rose
train
note
fair
pound
plant
box
saw

Hinky Pinkys

1. quick chick
2. sly guy
3. wee bee
4. yellow Jello
5. thick brick
6. fish dish
7. Swiss miss
8. sly fly
9. glad dad
10. fair hare

1. an upset thief
2. an angry employer
3. a stupid cleanser
4. a boat with no lights
5. a plant rainstorm
6. tinted footwear
7. an unhappy piece of wood
8. honest twins
9. delightful frozen water
10. a piece of furniture without life

Word Wizards

Word Wizard 1

1. downtown
2. right guard
3. square meal
4. cover up
5. Chicken Little
6. in the clear
7. too much too soon
8. wish upon a star
9. 32°
10. standing ovation
11. Frankenstein
12. Keep it under your hat.

Word Wizard 2

1. wake up
2. backyard
3. long underwear
4. weather forecast
5. hiccup
6. too much to eat
7. Dinner is on the table.
8. down in front
9. touchdown
10. square meal
11. just a little bit more
12. head over heels

Word Wizard 3

1. falling star
2. tomorrow
3. double dare
4. from floor to ceiling
5. ship to shore
6. split level
7. man overboard
8. pain in the neck
9. side step
10. parachutes
11. just for me
12. peace on Earth

Word Wizard 4

1. lemonade
2. bending over backward
3. boxing
4. deer crossing
5. three on three
6. high school
7. backward flip
8. double vision
9. look in the mirror
10. side by side
11. little Miss Muffet
12. one too many

Word Wizard 5

1. farmer in the dell
2. stay after school
3. drive-in movie
4. neon sign
5. catch up (or ketchup)
6. lefty
7. double agent
8. right price
9. top hat
10. left turn
11. winding down
12. six feet underground

Word Wizard 6

1. crossroads
2. lean over backward
3. go underground
4. double or nothing
5. merry-go-round
6. keep in touch
7. starfish
8. parakeets
9. wagon train
10. not up to par
11. side step
12. three little pigs

Word Wizard 7

1. right away
2. once over lightly
3. tricycle
4. batter up
5. Big Bird
6. one in a million
7. round trip ticket
8. double talk
9. pickup truck
10. please be on time
11. hyena
12. between meal snack

Word Wizard 8

1. formula
2. time after time
3. checkout counter
4. high chair
5. tulips
6. Who's on first?
7. home on the range
8. information
9. double trouble
10. slow down
11. partridge in a pear (pair) tree
12. water over the dam

Word Wizard 9

1. order in the court
2. make it up
3. banana split
4. double header
5. I'll get to it
6. face to face
7. Go jump in the lake.
8. four score and seven years
9. walk on water
10. low key
11. growing pains
12. four seasons

Word Wizard 10

1. lemon lime
2. hole in one
3. Little League
4. too good to be true
5. just in time
6. split ends
7. sunny side up
8. foreman
9. pizza with everything on it
10. hold up
11. valentine
12. tonight

Analogies

Classifications 1

1. parts of a volcano
2. things to wear on your feet
3. forms of precipitation
4. types of trees
5. Southwestern states
6. parts of a plant
7. rainforest animals
8. facial pairs
9. gases
10. building materials

Classifications 2

1. types of movement
2. animals
3. parts of a window
4. shades of red
5. central areas in a town
6. names for human fingers
7. parts of a bird
8. cutting tools
9. times of the day
10. cities in Pennsylvania

Classifications 3

1. things water does
2. natural disasters
3. ways to hit something
4. places where animals live
5. types of stone
6. names for cooking areas
7. types of outerwear
8. adhesives
9. types of happiness
10. Native American tribes

Classifications 4

1. birds
2. roads
3. temperatures
4. words that describe not being careful
5. train cars
6. parts of a shirt
7. celestial objects
8. collective nouns for groups of animals
9. musical terms
10. ways of yelling

Which Doesn't Belong? 1

1. Chicago
2. Santa Fe
3. St. Louis
4. Minneapolis
5. Oregon
6. Ohio
7. Missouri
8. Idaho

Which Doesn't Belong? 2

1. thunderstorms
2. cape
3. grazing
4. geothermal
5. valley
6. ocean
7. province
8. route

Which Doesn't Belong? 3

1. nerve
2. retina
3. creamy
4. fingernail
5. shark
6. compound eyes
7. cell wall
8. oak

Which Doesn't Belong? 4

1. soil
2. mountain
3. frost
4. Earth
5. solar energy
6. slate
7. series
8. tornado

Nonsense Groups 1

fir
mold

Nonsense Groups 2

dm
ice

Nonsense Groups 3

Mammoth Cave
Huron

Nonsense Groups 4

Prime Meridian
sound

Type by Type 1

1. S
2. S
3. A
4. S
5. A
6. S
7. S
8. A
9. A
10. S

Type by Type 2

1. S
2. S
3. A
4. S
5. S
6. A
7. A
8. S
9. S
10. A

Type by Type 3

1. PO
2. PO
3. KO
4. KO
5. PO
6. KO
7. PO
8. PO
9. KO
10. PO

ANSWER KEY

Type by Type 4

1. PO
2. KO
3. KO
4. PO
5. PO
6. KO
7. PO
8. KO
9. PO
10. PO

Completions 1

1. fish
2. <32°F
3. dusk
4. gases
5. Michigan
6. stalk
7. Treasure State
8. gills

Completions 2

1. seismograph
2. Atlantic
3. erosion
4. Juneau
5. marble
6. climatology
7. apples
8. igneous

Completions 3

1. reptile
2. Cape of Good Hope
3. evergreen
4. mouth
5. Bay
6. food
7. weigh
8. insect

Completions 4

1. Pacific
2. 0°C
3. Philippines
4. water
5. antler
6. wedge
7. southwest
8. element

NOTES

NOTES

NOTES